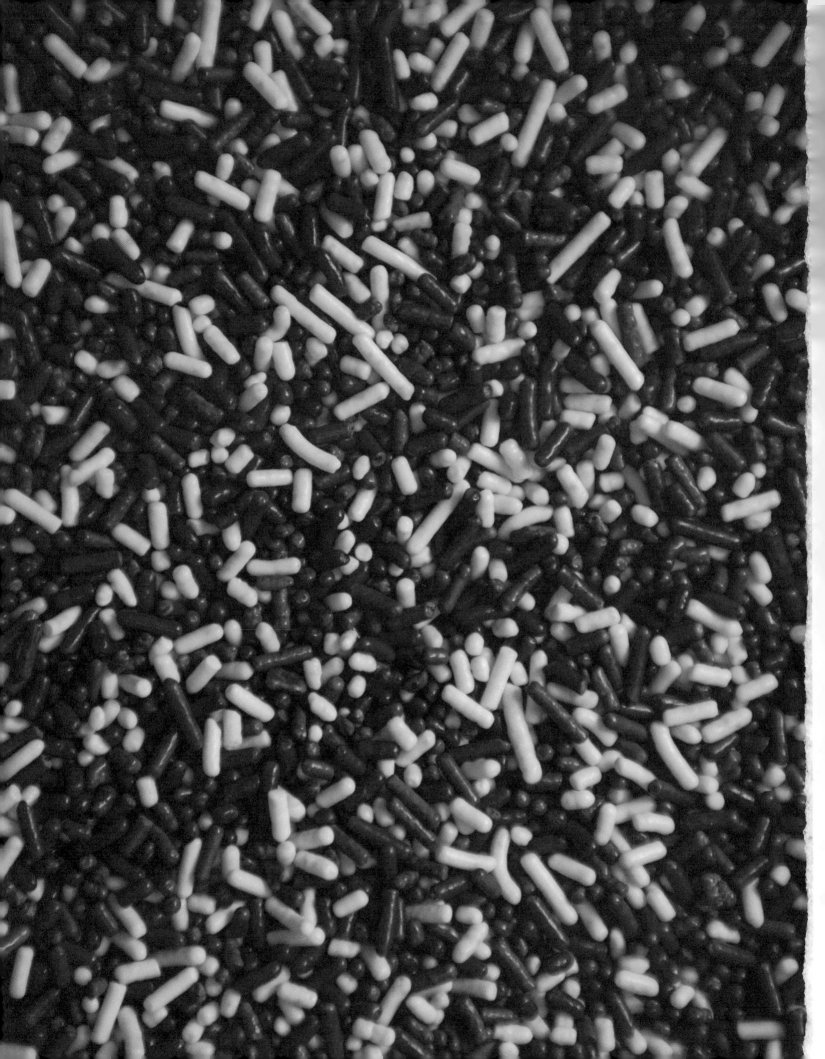

THE BIG BOOK OF
KING CAKE

THE BIG BOOK OF KING CAKE

THE STORIES & BAKERS BEHIND NEW ORLEANS' SWEETEST TRADITION

Matt Haines

Photography by Randy Krause Schmidt
Foreword by Liz Williams

SUSAN SCHADT PRESS

FOREWORD

To our credit New Orleanians are actively attentive about our historic food. This means we often look to our past when we evaluate the food we eat today and when we imagine its future. But sometimes we forget that the reason our food remains vital, interesting, and most of all delicious, is because it is constantly changing. It changes because of new people moving to the city with their own ideas and traditions, and it changes because of new ideas from locals and from advancements in technology. We must not forget that change can bring wonderful results.

Perhaps no New Orleans food better exemplifies this than the millennia-old king cake. The king cake has undergone its fair share of change over recent decades, but that doesn't stop the city from gobbling up as much as possible each Carnival season. Given the amount eaten, isn't it better if each foray can be different from the one before? Today we can find sushi king cake, ice cream king cake, king cake-flavored vodka, and more. How can we possibly complain about that, especially when we acknowledge these innovations are motivated by a love for, and celebration of, our favorite Carnival treat?

Lots of interesting questions are answered by author Matt Haines in *The Big Book of King Cake*. Where and why did the cake originate? Why do we hide a baby inside? What does the colored sugar represent? What does it mean to be "traditional" and does it matter? What is the king cake's future?

He also includes an historical progression and that allows us all to start at the same place. But unlike other writers who quibble over the king cake's changes, Matt makes the exploration of today's versions a joyful experience in which we all want to take part. That's what really makes this book special. It's forward-looking, optimistic, and epic in its inclusiveness of seventy-five bakers eager to share their expertise and their stories—a celebration of the current state of king cake, captured forever in this legacy publication.

The Big Book of King Cake is visually stunning and beautiful to read, but most of all it's the perfect antidote to the long wait after Mardi Gras day until the next January 6, when the season starts all over again.

— Liz Williams
Founder, Southern Food & Beverage Museum

INTRODUCTION

My hope is this book serves as both an ode to the bakers who make this historic cake, and a treasured, well-worn guide for those of us who love it so much.

Imagine this. You're living five thousand years ago in ancient Rome, the precursor to one of history's most legendary empires. Children are singing and everyone you see is smiling because you're about to celebrate what poet Gaius Valerius Catullus called "the best of times."

It's the Saturnalia. Businesses, courts, and schools all close. Sacrificed animals are served with other decadent, fatty foods in what amounts to a citywide feast. During this continuous celebration that can last a week, you and your fellow Romans eat too much, drink too much, sing songs, play games, and swap out your everyday togas for silly, brightly colored costumes. You grab a piece of cake, and you notice your slice has a bean inside. Lucky you! You're crowned queen or king for the day.

Now stop pretending. If you're a New Orleanian, or if you've visited our special city during those magical weeks between Twelfth Night and Fat Tuesday, then much of this likely sounds familiar. The music, the eating, the drinking. The laughter, the costumes, and, of course, the cake. The cake's become one of my favorite parts, because here in New Orleans it means so much more than just cake. It's tradition, it's experimentation, it's decadence, it's skill, it's community, and it's celebration.

My love for the king cake began in January 2017. I'd just been dumped, which as we all know, is fertile ground for boneheaded ideas. Looking for a distraction, I vowed to sample every king cake in New Orleans before Fat Tuesday. I didn't succeed, but I did eat more than eighty different kinds, and what struck me as amazing (besides that I didn't develop diabetes) was how many different varieties of king cake there are.

Those varieties include classic king cakes made with only brioche and colored sugar from recipes pushing one hundred years old. But they also include king cakes from those eager to infuse ancient customs with their own unique stories. Whether it's a Honduran with a love for guava, or a Yankee with an eye for flowers, a growing diversity means king cake is evolving faster than it ever has.

Is that a good thing or a bad thing? There are a lot of passionate opinions out there, and we're going to explore them all in this big book of king cake. Most of our time is spent near New Orleans, but we'll also make a few trips both around the state and across the globe. Along our journey, we'll tell the history of this special cake, share the stories of seventy-five extraordinary bakers who make them, and consider what this all means for one of the world's most unique cities. I hope you'll join us.

Chapter I

LOUISIANA LEGENDS

As mentioned in the Introduction, the predecessor to king cake was central to ancient Rome's Saturnalia festival. But how did king cake migrate from the feasts of the pagan world to the bakeries of Catholic Louisiana all these millennia later? Its journey began with the growth of the Roman Empire, eventually stretching from Great Britain in the west to Syria in the east. As the empire spread, so too did its traditions. In fact, those traditions proved more resilient than its host, surviving across the continent even after Rome's collapse in 476 AD.

With the rise of Christianity in Europe, church leaders decided they'd be better off adapting many of Rome's old pagan customs than eliminating them. King cake survived. Except instead of using the cake to honor the sun as the Romans had, European Catholics used it to celebrate the Epiphany, or the night—twelve days after his birth—that the son of God was revealed to the world through those three gift-giving kings.

When European colonization of New Orleans began in the eighteenth century, many early settlers were from Catholic-dominated areas like Spain and the Basque region of southern France. They brought their traditions with them, including their particular versions of king cake. Those cakes were brioche, ring-shaped, topped with colorful fruit, and stuffed with a fève such as a bean. The Spanish called their cake a roscón de reyes, while the southern French called theirs a gâteau de rois. In both cases the translation was "cake of kings."

Over time, traditions were altered, as they always are. The brioche became sweeter, the colorful fruit became colored sugar, and the bean became a plastic baby. We'll investigate these changes and more throughout the book, but it's unmistakable these cakes are the forefathers to the king cakes found in hundreds of New Orleans-area bakeries today.

As recently as fifty years ago, however, it wasn't hundreds of bakeries that carried the king cake, but only a handful. This chapter focuses on these *Louisiana Legends*, familiar names like McKenzie's, Randazzo's, Gambino's, and Haydel's, that baked king cakes at a time when they were selling only a fraction of the hundreds of thousands enjoyed today.

McKenzie's Pastry Shoppes by Tastee Donuts

"There's so much history in this cake."

Among New Orleanians born in the twentieth century, there is no mistaking a McKenzie's king cake. No layer of icing, no braided dough, no hint of cinnamon—just a simple, delicious, slightly sweetened brioche dough with purple, green, and gold sugar. You can trace the origins of king cake back thousands of years to the pagans of ancient Rome, but if you're looking for the grandfather of the modern day Louisiana-style king cake, McKenzie's is it. "There's so much history in this cake," said Lynda Santopadre, who, with her husband, founded Tastee Donuts, the company that now owns the McKenzie's name and its recipes.

That history is twofold. Not only did the McKenzie's king cake originate decades before other modern-day king cakes, but for generations of locals it also has a personal history. Nearly every one of the locally born bakers I spoke

The McKenzie's king cake with the brand's familiar slogan and recognizable logo.

with said their first king cake was from this once ubiquitous bakery.

Henry McKenzie founded the first McKenzie's Pastry Shoppe in 1929 on Prytania Street, eventually moving a few doors upriver to where The Creole Creamery ice cream shop now operates, displaying the McKenzie's lighted sign to this day. Henry struggled to keep the bakery profitable through the Depression and his former boss, Daniel Entringer bought him out in 1936 for just eighty-three dollars. He kept Henry as head baker and retained the shop's name after his wife correctly noted no one could confidently pronounce "Entringer."

The Entringer family—first Daniel, then his son Donald—built McKenzie's into a fifty-four store empire that would popularize sweet treats like buttermilk drops, turtle cookies and, of course, king cake. The bakery reportedly made their first king cake when a Carnival krewe requested one for its ball. They wouldn't stop baking them for decades; though, in those first years, McKenzie's was lucky to sell a half-dozen. By the time McKenzie's closed its doors in May 2000, the city abounded with different varieties, but none were like that tri-colored, bready brioche classic. At its height, the bakery sold more than three hundred and fifty thousand king cakes annually and was responsible for not only the popularity of the cake, but for its tri-color sugar and plastic baby fève, as well.

Fortunately, the recipe wasn't lost upon McKenzie's closing. Tastee Donuts purchased the rights and still makes the cake each Carnival season. "We couldn't let such an important part of New Orleans history fade away," Lynda said. "This is the king cake that started it all."

LEFT PHOTOS: The traditional McKenzie's king cake is known for its simplicity. **RIGHT PHOTOS:** Tastee Donuts also makes more modern varieties such as the buttermilk drop king cake (top) and the donut king cake made with Tastee's donut dough.

Cartozzo's Bakery

"When I first suggested icing, my grandpa said, 'That's not king cake! It's a cinnamon roll!' Can you imagine if he could see king cake now?"

Now that king cakes come in flavors like boudin, peanut butter whiskey, and sushi, it's easy to forget even basic filled king cakes like cream cheese and strawberry are a relatively recent invention. It's a trend that popularized among New Orleans' bakeries in the 1980s, but many consider Angelo Cartozzo to be the movement's founder.

Angelo's grandfather, also an Angelo, opened his bakery in 1969 with Dick Bruce, the legendary spokesman for many of McKenzie's Pastry Shoppes' most famous commercials. A young Angelo, just seven years old, worked there, washing pans and making fig cookies. "I learned so much from my grandfather," Angelo said. "He made all his fillings and products from scratch and never cut corners. Not many bakeries do that anymore." Angelo remembered going to school and teaching the lunch ladies how to make cinnamon rolls like his grandfather did. "They sold a lot more after I taught them!"

Two employees and bakery owner Angelo Cartozzo with his traditional king cake.

in the 1970s to top sweet-dough king cakes with icing, the boy suggested they follow the trend. His grandfather didn't agree. "He said, 'That's not king cake! It's a cinnamon roll!'" Angelo laughed. "Can you imagine if he could see king cake now?"

But Angelo didn't always follow trends. Sometimes he spearheaded them. After his grandfather passed away, he and his family opened Frances' Bakery, named after his mother. One morning around Carnival in 1983, he and his brother were filling Danishes. "My brother looked at me and asked, 'What if we put these fillings inside the king cake?'" They flipped over their traditional king cake, poked holes in the bottom, and pumped some Bavarian cream inside. "Our mom tried it and was like, 'What?!' and told us, 'Make six more right now.'" They've been making them ever since; the only changes being they now bake the filling inside the cake, and they offer a lot more filling options.

Angelo wasn't done innovating. Back then, most grocery stores didn't have their own bakery departments, so they'd contract with a local shop to set up inside the store. McKenzie's was a common fixture, but Frances' had opened inside several Schwegmann's, including one in Slidell. Soon, however, grocery chains began developing their own bakeries. "They didn't need us anymore, but we had a lot of customers

A couple of years later, Grandpa Angelo looked to move into a better location but lacked the money. Fortunately, he was well connected. His friend, Carlos Marcello offered to lend him $50,000 to open a new shop, Angelo's Bakery. (Marcello was the longtime leader of the New Orleans Mafia, but that's a story for a different book.)

The younger Angelo, now a teenager, was often at the new bakery. He was there when his grandfather invented the Turkish Macaroon, a favorite of actress Elizabeth Taylor that she sometimes had shipped to herself in Las Vegas. And, during Carnival, he helped his grandpa make king cakes. "Back then it was basically just this yellow-white bread dough with sugar on it," Angelo recalled. When it became popular

OPPOSITE PAGE: A praline king cake from Cartozzo's Bakery. TOP PHOTO: Angelo holds a framed *Times-Picayune* article from 1990 about how Frances' Bakery created the first drive-in king cake shop. The article includes a photo of his father Henry (right), Angelo (center), and his brother Tony. RIGHT PHOTO: The muffuletta king cake is a popular savory option from Cartozzo's.

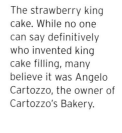

The strawberry king cake. While no one can say definitively who invented king cake filling, many believe it was Angelo Cartozzo, the owner of Cartozzo's Bakery.

and former staff on the Northshore who loved our products, especially our king cakes," Angelo said, "so I told them I'd ship to them." He worked with FedEx® to create boxes to mail king cakes. Today, hundreds of thousands of king cakes are shipped around the world each year from dozens of New Orleans bakeries. "As far as I know, it started with us."

By 1990, Angelo started his own bakery, Cartozzo's, to meet the unmet demand he saw for wholesale baked goods. They sell breads, rolls, pistolettes, and more to casinos, restaurants, and hotels around the state. But, of course, they still make king cake, a business that's grown from three thousand cakes per year at Frances' to one hundred thousand today. Angelo's proud that he's helped advance this local tradition over the years. "Everything can be improved," he said, "and it might upset people who say, 'That's not king cake!' or whatever, but look at king cake now. Filling is everywhere. Sometimes changes stick."

Cannata's

"The world's full of mass-produced products. We prefer that king cake isn't one of them. Variety takes more time, but it lets us share something new and personal with our customers."

The story of this renowned Houma, Louisiana, bakery began in 1939 when Vincent Cannata and Fannie Canale got married. Each grew up in Italian households with parents who owned small New Orleans corner groceries. As a child, Vincent milked the family's cows and delivered that milk door to door. Already an entrepreneur, he realized he could increase business if he offered more goods, so he scoured the French Market for fresh fruit, vegetables, and bread to sell.

That's how Vincent met Fannie, delivering produce to her father's market where she worked. So when the two eventually married, staying in the produce business made sense. They opened a fruit stand together, eighty-five miles west in Morgan City. Vincent picked up produce from the French Market each day, and

TOP-LEFT PHOTO: Vince Cannata (left) and his sister Joni run the business their parents opened almost eighty years ago. Vince is holding the Ti-Can Pecan king cake, as well as locally made bourbon used in the cake from Bayou Terrebonne Distillers. Joni is holding an Italian Chantilly king cake. **BOTTOM-RIGHT:** The Rougagooey king cake raises money to support efforts by the South Louisiana Wetlands Discovery Center to preserve the Louisiana coast.

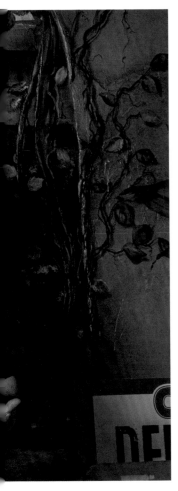

Fannie often had it sold before her husband got it back to the store.

Business boomed, and the fruit stand eventually turned into their first supermarket. In 1972, with a family in tow, they opened another grocery in Houma with a full bakery. But it wasn't until 1989, under the direction of Vincent and Fannie's children, Vince and Joni, that the bakery took on a life of its own.

"In '89 we did this big expansion that finally allowed us to bake the variety and volume we wanted from scratch," Vince explained. That ambition is easy to see in Cannata's king cakes. Over the years, they've baked more than sixty flavors. Joni's the mastermind behind most of them, and her creativity aligns with how the siblings do business. "The world's full of mass-produced products," Vince said. "We prefer that king cake isn't one of them. Variety takes more time, but it lets us share something new and personal with our customers."

Some aspects of their process stay consistent no matter the variety. There's disagreement among bakers over whether to fill king cakes before or after baking them. Vince and Joni are adamant that filling first is key to their success, which includes a New Orleans King Cake Festival "People's Choice Award" for their Gooey Butter Snickerdoodle king cake. "Filling the cake first let's all that flavor bake in," Vince explained. That's one of many things they've learned over the years.

Another is the importance of community. "Terrebone Parish is such a rich and beautiful

Cannata's makes more than sixty varieties of king cake, including the Rougagooey (top-left), the traditional (top-center), the Italian Chantilly (top-right), the Ti-Can Pecan (bottom-left), the Tigerrrr (middle-bottom), and the Who Dat (previous page, top-right).

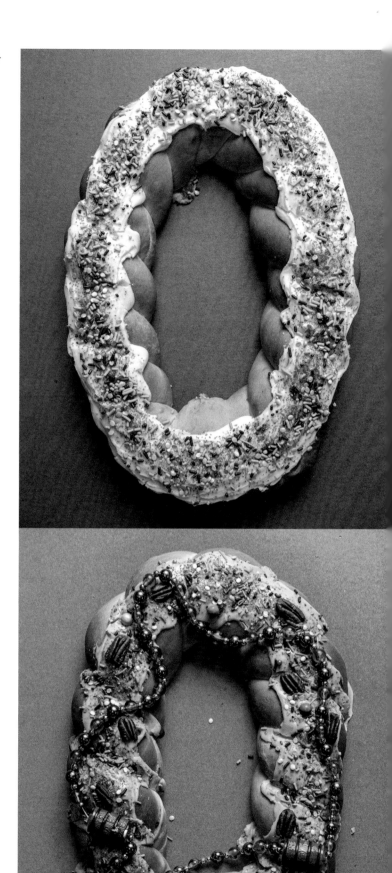

place," Vince said, "and we're proud to call it home, so we do what we can to support it." The Rougarou Fest, for example, was voted one of the "Top 10 Costume Parties in America" by *USA Today*. The festival, which honors the frightening Rougarou (basically, a Cajun Bigfoot) raises money for the South Louisiana Wetlands Discovery Center, a local nonprofit working to preserve the rapidly eroding Louisiana coast. But when the coronavirus pandemic forced last year's festival to downsize, Cannata's created their Rougagooey king cake and donated portions of the proceeds to the Discovery Center's preservation efforts. Similarly, Vince said, their "Hum 'M' Bird" king cake raises

money for the Mary Bird Cancer Center, "so our fellow residents don't need to travel far for the treatment they need."

Cannata's even makes collaboration king cakes with other community businesses. Their "Ti-Can Pecan" king cake uses whiskey from Bayou Terrebonne Distillers, the only whiskey made exclusively with Louisiana corn. "Our parents were deeply connected to the communities in which they operated their stores," Vince smiled. "It must be in our blood."

If you don't have time to travel to Houma, have no fear. Cannata's king cakes are available in New Orleans at the King Cake Hub. (You really should visit Houma sometime soon, though!)

Nonna Randazzo's Bakery

"There are lots of opinions on what a king cake is. To us and our customers, this is king cake."

What makes a king cake king cake? If you ask seventy-five bakers, you'll get seventy-five answers. (Trust me!) Each is valid, but when king cake royalty like the Randazzo family gives their opinion, I'm taking notes.

"First, you can't just make an oval ring of dough. King cakes are braided," insisted Joel Randazzo Forjet, daughter of Lawrence Randazzo, one of three brothers who started the original Randazzo's Hi-Lan Bakery in 1965. Next, she said, it needs purple, green, and gold

sugar. "But the sugar goes below the icing," Joel emphasized, an approach only the Randazzo family and a few other bakeries take. She said putting the sugar on top of the icing makes it too crunchy. Plus, at Nonna Randazzo's the icing is reserved for nonpareils. The other Randazzo family bakeries top their icing with sprinkles instead, but not Joel. "My dad and uncles used nonpareils at Hi-Lan, so that's how we do it here."

Sticking to tradition is important to Joel because, for her customers, this is one of the few places to get treats like shoe soles, petit fours, Russian cake, and Italian macarons that taste how they remember. Joel can relate. So many of her life's milestones involve her family's bakery. She remembers helping decorate king

TOP PHOTO: (from left to right) Co-owners Felix Forjet Jr. and Joel Randazzo Forjet, their son Felix III, and his wife Kayla.

cakes even when she was so young she could barely reach the table. She remembers being in high school one Carnival when her dad, short-staffed, said, "Call that boy you're dating to help!" That boy, now her husband, has been working in the king cake business with her ever since. And she remembers, years later, when her son was born only days before Mardi Gras. "I was alone in the hospital because the whole family was making king cakes," she laughed. "At least they brought me one!"

Joel acknowledged some may disagree with her specific idea of what makes a king cake.

"I'm sure someone will say ours isn't king cake because we sell holiday versions year-round, or because we put the sugar under the icing, or because we have crazy flavors like tiramisu. But that's okay. We make them like we always have. To my parents, me, my husband, my kids, my grandkids, and our customers, this is king cake."

TOP PHOTOS: Felix Forjet III prepares king cakes, including braiding the dough. **OPPOSITE PAGE:** Nonna Randazzo's offers king cakes year-round that include several seasonal varieties. **NEXT SPREAD:** Their award-winning tiramisu king cake is one of the most delicious king cakes I've tasted.

The Bean

I once walked into my office break room to find a coworker stuffing the plastic baby they'd found back into the king cake. "Have you no shame?" I thought. To be fair, unless you're a child excited about becoming royalty for the day, why would you want to find the baby? All you get is the responsibility to buy the next cake. But this wasn't always the case. Before there was a baby, there was a bean, and the bean was coveted.

In ancient Greece, for example, real leaders were chosen by tallying actual votes cast with beans. Over in Rome, even being a mock "King for the Day" had real perks. The king or queen—often, but not always, a young child—could give orders to their subjects and preside over the festivities. (If finding the baby meant I could pick the party's food and set its playlist, I'd find that baby every time.)

Equally significant to the bean's value is what it symbolized. To those ancient pagans, the bean was considered magical. The story of Jack and the Beanstalk, in which magic beans led to a giant's treasure, can be traced back more than six thousand years! But as Christianity swept across Europe, the bean went from magical to blessed. Being "King for the Day," now predicted good luck and fortune. The French idiom, "Il a trouvé la fève au gâteau!" is still used any time someone makes a lucky discovery, but the translation, "He has found the bean in the cake!" refers specifically to king cake.

There are even a few examples in modern New Orleans of the bean's significance. The woman who receives the bean at the annual ball of the Twelfth Night Revelers is crowned the krewe's queen. And several local bakeries have returned to hiding a bean or nut inside their cake instead of a baby. Mae's Bakeshop, for example, adds local flare by using a red bean.

Can a return to tradition revive the importance of finding a favor inside the cake? If you find yourself king or queen for the day this Carnival season, command your fellow partygoers to make it so.

Gambino's Bakery

"Bakeries like ours create memories. We baked your wedding cake, your grandma's birthday cake, your mom's birthday cake, your birthday cake, and now your daughter's birthday cake. It's special when a community bakery can provide that kind of continuity."

If your nickname is The King of King Cakes, you've got to be doing something big. Gambino's Bakery most definitely is, shipping hundreds of thousands of king cakes each season to recipients as diverse as Disney World, hotels, and Tulane University alumni scattered across the country and yearning for a slice of Carnival.

But at the heart of their impressive operation, The King of King Cakes is still a mom-and-pop shop. "I think people yearn for the butcher, the baker, and the candlestick maker," said Vincent Scelfo, Gambino's owner. "Bakeries like ours create memories. We baked your wedding cake, your

grandma's birthday cake, your mom's birthday cake, your birthday cake, and now your daughter's birthday cake. It's special when a community bakery can provide that kind of continuity."

As one of the oldest operations in the area, Gambino's has thrived on that continuity. The business began nearly one hundred years ago, in the early 1920s, when Beulah Ledner baked treats for Tulane and Newcomb College students out of her Uptown home. Beulah became a legend when she invented the multi-layered doberge cake before selling the company and recipes to Joe Gambino in 1946 after she struggled with health issues.

Vincent's father, Sam, was an employee at Gambino's, and he purchased the bakery with his friend Joe Paternostro in 1978. "My dad still works here today," Vincent said. "It's the definition of a family-run bakery. My mom works here, my wife works here, and my two kids work here when they want to make a few dollars. They'll be the next owners. I don't understand building something just to sell it off."

The Scelfos have always looked to improve,

RIGHT PHOTO: The locally famous sign in front of Gambino's Bakery on Veterans Memorial Boulevard. Gambino's has served the area for nearly a century, originally under a different name. Before it was purchased by Joe Gambino in 1946, the business was called "Beulah Ledner Bakery," named after its founder and the inventor of the doberge cake.

even as their business approaches the century mark. Early on, they switched from a dry brioche dough to a sweeter Danish dough, an innovation several bakeries were toying with at the time. That led to another successful experiment. "We sold Danishes at the shop, and nobody comes in to buy plain Danishes," Vincent said. "They want them filled. So we tried adding those same fillings to our Danish dough king cake and people loved it." Today, the Gambino's team continues to make improvements, seeking out better ingredients, creating a more welcoming shop, and even adding new flavors to their king cake portfolio. "We really feed off the creativity

OPPOSITE PAGE, MIDDLE-RIGHT PHOTO: Gambino's is one of the few bakeries that still bakes its babies directly into the cake. Many have stopped the practice for fear of choking hazards, or at least liability concerns. **BOTTOM-LEFT PHOTO:** The bakery twists its king cake dough, an alternative to braiding. **BOTTOM-RIGHT PHOTO:** Always seeking ways to innovate, the Gambino's team bakes their dough in boxes that make it easier to ship without damaging their finished king cake.

coming from the city's smaller bakeries," Vincent explained. "I love going to Breads on Oak, Celtica, and others to see what they're doing. Those visits push us to try new things, like a recent Nutella® king cake we made."

Vincent believes if they continue to improve quality, longevity will be the result. That's not only important to his family, but to his customers, as well. "Every New Orleanian knows places that 'Ain't dere no more,'" he said, using the local colloquialism for beloved institutions now closed, "but families have been coming to Gambino's for their birthday doberge, or their Thanksgiving dessert, or their king cake for decades. These aren't just cakes. They're memories."

Soon the home bakeshop-turned-King will have created one hundred years' worth of those memories. But Vincent said they won't stop there. "We're going for another hundred years after that. At least!"

Haydel's Bakery

"The tradition is supposed to be whoever finds the baby brings the next cake. But, by high school, the new rule was 'Haydel brings his king cake every week!'"

Despite having such a famous bakery surname, Ryan Haydel's king cake story starts the same as that of a lot of New Orleans kids. "Some of the first king cakes I remember eating were Fridays at school," he said. For decades in local schools, Fridays during Carnival season have been synonymous with the king cake party. To this day, Ryan said cake sales spike at Haydel's Bakery on Thursday afternoons and Friday mornings as parents of children responsible for this week's king cake scramble to pick one up.

Ryan is a third-generation baker and co-owner of the bakery his grandfather founded in 1959. For many, it's the pinnacle of king cake: a sweeter, modern option for those seeking an alternative to the versions without icing that came before. In the 1980s, when Ryan was a child, the majority of New Orleanians were still eating McKenzie's. "Especially if you were buying a king cake for your child's third grade class," Ryan explained. "There was a McKenzie's in every neighborhood, and you could get a huge cake very cheap." But when it was Ryan's turn to bring a king cake to school, he'd make one at his family's bakery with modern adaptations like sweet dough and

Kindergarteners at Homer A. Plessy Community School obviously enjoying this traditional king cake from Haydel's Bakery.

icing. "Pretty soon teachers, who I remember loving our cake, set it up so I was always the first person to bring the king cake each Carnival." But it didn't end there. The student who finds the baby is supposed to bring next week's cake, but by high school, that custom vanished in Ryan's classes. "The new rule was, 'Haydel brings his king cake every week!'"

As Ryan grew up, so did his family's business, which his father and uncle transformed into one of New Orleans' premier bakeries. Today Haydel's sells as many as ninety thousand king cakes each year. "Looking back, they were just so smart about the expert bakers they surrounded themselves with and the innovations they pursued," Ryan said. In the late-1980s, for example, Haydel's was one of the first bakeries to ship king cakes across the country. Today, they ship twenty thousand annually.

Haydel's innovations also extended to how they marketed themselves. "My dad once donated a king cake so big it wrapped around my school's auditorium," Ryan laughed. It's a feat that seemed unbeatable until the Haydel's team set a Guinness Book world record in 2010, wrapping two king cakes around the Louisiana Superdome! Combined, the cakes were more than a mile long, weighed in excess of four tons, and were the equivalent of more than three thousand, two hundred and fifty regular-sized king cakes. "Most importantly," Ryan said, "it raised $47,000 for breast cancer research. It's important we give back to our community, because it's our home and we love it here."

Watch how New Orleanians react when a Haydel's king cake is brought into a party or classroom, and you'll see this city loves Haydel's Bakery right back.

Haydel's Bake Shop General Manager Kerrin Barras shows the kindergarteners how to ice a king cake. Minutes later, she allowed the students to decorate the cake with colored sugar. Chaos ensued.

Chapter 2
TRADITIONS

In New Orleans, king cake is more than just cake. It's also tradition, with residents attaching annual customs to their favorite Carnival treat. Examples include not eating the cake until Twelfth Night, its familiar ring shape, the purple, green, and gold sugar, and of course, the favor hidden inside. These king cake traditions were established in New Orleans generations before Carnival, brought to the city by French and Spanish Catholics beginning in the 1700s. The church associated the cake with Twelfth Night so each year on January 6, Creole families of French and Spanish descent ate king cake and crowned their royalty.

Carnival and Mardi Gras customs were established later, in the middle decades of the nineteenth century. This slowly helped raise the king cake's profile. As formal parading krewes like Comus, Rex, and the Twelfth Night Revelers were formed, king cake became a feature of many of their Carnival season balls and thrust the culinary tradition into public view. Beginning in the 1870s, for example, local newspapers reported on the Twelfth Night Revelers' annual January 6 celebration. They'd tell of the elaborate, multi-tiered "king's cake"—more like the fondant-covered Twelfth Night Cakes of England—and the New Orleans debutantes who received the gold and silver beans that transformed them into a queen and maids, respectively. The Twelfth Night Revelers' yearly ball continues to this day. So does the tradition of king cake, but not only for Carnival krewes. The student who finds the baby in their classroom's cake is also crowned royalty, if just for the day.

While reading about the bakers featured in this chapter, we'll see that traditions related to king cake and the Carnival season come in all shapes and sizes. We'll learn how one of New Orleans' oldest restaurants revised one of its most popular rituals, how a family of Vietnamese refugees found a new home with the help of a decades-old king cake style, and how a James Beard award-winning chef tapped into his familial history to create a new king cake recipe only he could imagine.

Galatoire's Restaurant

"We have families that have dined here for generations. They each have their own culinary customs and rituals with us, whether it's the days they regularly come or the appetizers they order."

Founded more than three hundred years ago, New Orleans is full of traditions. Few institutions exemplify that better than Bourbon Street restaurant Galatoire's. Since its opening in 1905, Galatoire's has won a James Beard award for Outstanding Restaurant in America, was mentioned in playwright Tennessee Williams' *A Streetcar Named Desire*, and has hosted scores of celebrities and even presidents. "It's impossible to count the number of traditions honored here," said Galatoire's President Melvin Rodrigue. "We have families that have dined here for generations. They each have their own culinary customs and rituals with us, whether it's the days they regularly come or the appetizers they order."

But one tradition that's been shared by legions of New Orleanians across the decades is Friday lunch. It's the glorious weekly ritual that prompts hundreds of residents to leave work early to enjoy a decadent lunch of buttery escargot, oysters en brochette, bread pudding,

gin martinis, and whatever else their hearts desire. "When you come for Friday lunch, you have no intention of going back to work," Melvin explained. "I think it runs parallel to that joie de vivre you find in this city. New Orleans lives for the weekend and for so many New Orleanians, the weekend starts with Galatoire's."

One doesn't simply walk into Friday lunch. It's one of the most coveted events in town, and Galatoire's doesn't traditionally take reservations for the meal. Instead, New Orleanians cut their workdays even shorter to stand in line and secure a table. During their two most popular lunches of the year—the Fridays before Christmas and Mardi Gras—diners must arrive even earlier. Much earlier.

Costumed New Orleanians enjoy Galatoire's king cake while they wait in line for the restaurant's renowned Friday lunch.

"We've had people camping outside overnight. Some even got here on Tuesday," Melvin said, shaking his head. "That's admirable, but probably not sustainable." Galatoire's now accepts reservations for those two dates, breaking a long-standing rule.

To make something positive of the change, they turned it into a fundraiser that has raised more than $2.5 million for local charities.

For all this talk about tradition, it's hard to believe 2021 was Galatoire's first foray into the mother of all traditions: king cake. "We've occasionally made them for events," Melvin said, "but with the coronavirus pandemic, we wanted to have something special customers could pick up. King cake seemed perfect." Galatoire's cake is unfilled and topped with thick white icing and ribbons of green sugar. The colors might not be traditionally Carnival, but they've been Galatoire's for years.

Melvin's a big fan of his pastry team's cake, which is anchored by a flavorful, silky-smooth dough. He said the king cakes of his childhood—topped with only sugar—were too dry. Melvin welcomed the addition of icing but felt the subsequent push to add fillings was too much. "Call me conventional, but I want cinnamon, icing and sugar—that's it!" It's yet another tradition you can now find at the historic Galatoire's.

TOP PHOTOS: Executive Chef Phillip L. Lopez prepares Galatoire's king cake. Green and white are the French Quarter restaurant's colors, making a fitting combination for the cake's sugars, as well.

Blue Dot Donuts

"Our grandpa taught us it's important to be in touch with who you serve — to make it a personal thing."

"**I** bet this guy's getting a half dozen strawberry glazed," Zach Foster yelled across the shop to his brother Zane.

"That's an easy one," Zane shot back. "He gets that every day."

This is the kind of interaction the brothers often have before a customer walks into Blue Dot Donuts. Zach has owned the Mid-City shop since 2017, and he was head baker here for years before that. He and Zane take pride knowing their regulars' names and orders. "Our grandpa taught us it's important to be in touch with who you serve," Zach said. "To make it a personal thing."

He watched his grandpa do exactly that for years at his doughnut shop in Deer Lodge, Montana. They worked the overnight shift together with Zach's uncle. Even after "retiring," his grandpa sat in a recliner behind the counter and talked to the police officers, bartenders, and other third shifters placing late night orders. The shop had a family feel, and that's what Zach and Zane try to create at Blue Dot.

"It's all about love!" Zane laughed from behind the counter after giving his customer the predicted half dozen strawberry-glazed donuts.

One of Zach's first New Orleans jobs was making tens of thousands of king cakes at a local wholesale bakery. "My hands would be dyed purple from the sugar," he said. "I vowed I was done with king cake after that."

But no New Orleans baker is ever done with king cake. To stay sane, Zach limits the quantity, but focuses on higher quality. "To me, a great king cake is made in the dough," Zach said. "Our dough comes from our doughnuts and apple fritters. If you like those things, I think you'll love our king cake."

RIGHT PHOTO: Shop owner Zach Foster (right) and his brother Zane in front of Blue Dot Donuts. **NEXT PAGE:** Top-left, icing the apple fritter king cake; top-right, sprinkling green sugar on the maple bacon king cake; bottom-left, sprinkling gold sugar on the traditional donut king cake.

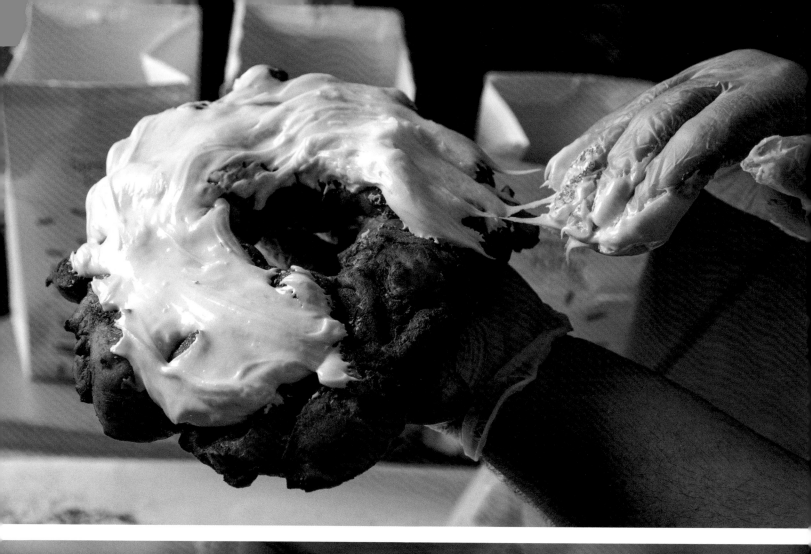

Bywater Bakery

"My first job was in a bakery back when I was fourteen years old. You had to be fifteen to work in Vermont, but I wanted the job so badly I lied about my age."

If you've eaten king cake more than once—and because you're holding this book you probably have—there's a good chance Chaya Conrad was responsible for at least one of them. Chaya's the owner of Bywater Bakery, home to a slate of king cakes consistently on just about every New Orleans "Best Of" list. But her king cake credentials began long before she opened her beloved bakery in 2017.

She worked up through the ranks of Whole Foods Market, becoming bakery manager at

their headquarters in Austin, Texas. Next, she spent eight years as bakery director at Louisiana's Rouses Markets where, suffice it to say, she dabbled in king cake. "If you're managing a bakery in New Orleans, you've got to be ready to make a lot of them," Chaya said, "but if you're working at a grocery store bakery, the numbers are mind-blowing." At Rouses that meant more than four hundred thousand king cakes per year!

But Chaya yearned for a bakery of her own. It's a dream she'd had for quite some time. "My first job was in a bakery back when I was fourteen years old," she said. "You had to be fifteen to work in Vermont, but I wanted the job so badly I lied about my age." She moved to New Orleans when she was eighteen, and apart from a few sporadic years, she's called the city home since. Chaya left Rouses when a Creole cottage in the heart of the Bywater neighborhood became available. This was the perfect place for her bakery. And it opened on the perfect day. The most important king cake day of the year— January 6, aka Twelfth Night. "Before we could even operate inside our shop, we were selling king cakes outside," she remembered.

And there's a consensus among New Orleanians that these are some great king cakes. The secret, Chaya said, is instead of using cinnamon in the dough like most bakers, Bywater Bakery uses an ooey-gooey butter smear. It gives the cake a mouthfeel people seem to appreciate, she said. "And, also, I just really love the taste of ooey-gooey butter!"

Bywater Bakery was dreamed up as a neighborhood bakery, a place where the community

LEFT PHOTO: Chaya Conrad with a slice of king cake in front of her bakery. **OPPOSITE PAGE:** The berry Chantilly king cake is a favorite at Bywater Bakery.

"Instead of cinnamon, we use an ooey-gooey butter smear that gives our king cakes a great mouthfeel. Also, I just really love the taste of ooey-gooey butter!"

would gather to celebrate birthdays and anniversaries. It's common to find local musicians performing at or around the piano or outside the bakery. The work of local artists fills the walls, and the menu is a diverse offering that includes Chaya's baked goods, Miss Linda's famous yakamein, bagels on Fridays, and much more.

Of course, during Carnival season, king cakes are the main attraction. You'd expect nothing less from a bakery born on Twelfth Night. In addition to their traditional "Carnival" king cake, Chaya bakes varieties such as Chantilly, bouille, Creole cream cheese, azul dulce blueberry, apple with brown sugar, praline, lemon cream, and a trio of savory options.

Whether you stop in for live music—including during Bywater Bakery's birthday and Twelfth Night Party—or have the cake shipped across the country, you're guaranteed one of New Orleans' favorite king cakes from one of its most treasured bakers.

TOP PHOTO: An ooey-gooey butter smear is applied to the king cake dough at Bywater Bakery. **OPPOSITE PAGE:** The bakery offers three varieties of savory king cakes, including this spinach and artichoke king cake topped with purple, green, and gold-colored parmesan cheese.

Caluda's King Cake

"Each Carnival we hire a team of seasonal employees. Some are seventy years old, sprinkling colored sugar. But I tell all of them, when they're making king cakes, they're ambassadors of New Orleans."

During Carnival season, John Caluda oversees the baking of two thousand king cakes each day. But he still remembers the first he ever tasted. It was in 1965 when he was in first grade. "I didn't like it," he laughed. "It looked like a piece of French bread with sugar on it!"

King cake has changed a lot over the decades. If you appreciate the unique fillings

today's bakers use, many believe John is to thank. "He's the first one I really saw getting creative like that," said Jean-Luc Albin, owner of Maurice French Pastries. In 1996, while the rest of the city had only recently acclimated to basic jelly and cream cheese king cakes, John was inventing the crawfish king cake using the same filling from his popular crawfish strudel sold at the New Orleans Jazz and Heritage Festival. And crawfish is just the tip of the iceberg. White chocolate bread pudding king cake, apple

flan king cake, cookie dough king cake, and approximately a trillion other options have customers lined up out the door. "It would be a lot easier if we just had three versions," said John's son, Josh, "but it's fun to see what people respond to."

In addition to the flavors, John believes his dough sets Caluda's king cakes apart. The recipe was a collaboration between him and Dianne Randazzo, former wife of renowned baker Manny Randazzo, Jr. The partnership

was originally named Dianne Randazzo's King Cakes, but a judge ruled their cakes couldn't carry the Randazzo name. "Randazzo's has a high-quality cake and ours has some similarities, but it's not the same," John explained. "Ours is lighter, fluffier, and intentionally not so moist." Caluda's achieves that by allowing their dough to ferment longer and by braiding the dough less tightly. "A lot of bakers don't braid anymore, but it's not just aesthetics. It also affects texture and flavor by situating the cinnamon, sugar, and

butter more evenly."

While many king cakes dry out after a single day, Caluda's are built to last. John and his team test that theory by leaving one in the break room for a week, or by freezing then thawing it three months later. John gives it a taste, and his reaction is notably different than when he tried his first slice almost sixty years ago. "Every time it surprises me, and I think 'Damn, we make a really good king cake here!'"

La Petite Sophie

"Like everything else at my bakery, I try to make king cakes I love to eat. I've never been a fan of those super-sweet king cakes covered in icing."

Like whole generations of New Orleanians, La Petite Sophie owner Jeff Becnel's earliest Carnival memories are of McKenzie's famous king cakes. He and his two brothers could finish an entire cake in a day, he said. "All the fresh ones were already sold, but it didn't really matter," Jeff explained. "You couldn't taste the difference with those McKenzie's cakes anyway."

Several decades later, an adult-Jeff places a far higher value on freshness. Your mouth is watering before you even walk into La Petite Sophie. You can smell the richness of his baked goods from the small bakery's parking lot. Inside you're met with several glass cases full of options, but if it's your first time in his Harahan bakeshop, you should start with what Jeff is known for— the viennoiseries. Invented in Vienna, but made famous by the French, it's a bridge between pastries and bread. Layered, famously flaky, and great for breakfast, croissants and brioche are two of the category's most popular types.

Jeff's path to baked goods was a windy one. He graduated from the Culinary Institute of America in 2004 and focused on savory cooking. "In the United States, pastries are kind of an afterthought," he said, "so I really didn't give them much energy." That all changed in 2009 when Jeff began a stint living and working in Europe. He spent time in England, France, and Italy, and said his mind was blown by the attention and detail paid to pastries.

Beginning with kouign amann and later focusing on croissants, he studied under some of the greats of European baking. Returning to the U.S., he continued to develop his skills in New York, where he perfected lamination, the process of creating layers of dough and butter that make viennoiseries light and flaky. Jeff opened La Petite Sophie in 2013, first as a pop-up at farmers markets and later with a brick-and-mortar location. The shop's king cakes reflect its owner's journey as a pastry chef.

Two of them are extremely popular in France during Carnival season. The galette

OPPOSITE PAGE: Top-left, Kouign amann king cake; top-right, gâteau des rois; bottom-right, strawberry and cream king cake; bottom-left, galette des rois. **RIGHT PHOTO:** Bakery owner Jeff Becnel (left) and baker Philip Patten with their king cakes. Traditionally, in France, whoever finds the fève in the galette des rois receives a paper crown to wear.

des rois is sold in several New Orleans bakeries and is ubiquitous across France. The gâteau des rois, on the other hand, is popular exclusively in southern France. While you're not likely to find a gâteau des rois in New Orleans outside of La Petite Sophie, it's this colorful, crown-shaped cake, likely brought here by late-nineteenth century immigrants from southern France, that helped inspire the New Orleans-style king cakes we know today.

But it's Jeff's kouign amann king cake that best reflects the marriage of the skills and tastes he developed in France to the New Orleans traditions he remembers from his childhood.

Cut in half you can see the flaky, buttery layers that are the product of his lamination. Look on top, however, and you'll find the same purple, gold, and green sugar Jeff would have seen on McKenzie's cakes as a child.

"Like everything else in my bakery, I try to make king cakes I love to eat," Jeff said. "I've never been a fan of those super-sweet king cakes covered in icing, but I do love kouign amann. I think my customers do, too."

TOP PHOTO: The gâteau des rois is southern France's version of king cake. It is much more difficult to find in New Orleans than the more common galette des rois of northern France.

Langenstein's

"Oh my gosh, my kids love it when I bring king cake home from work. That's what the king cake tradition is to them."

L
ike so many New Orleans households, there are certain traditions Meshawn Gresham's family upholds each Carnival. For example, they never miss the big parades like Bacchus and Endymion. And they've always got a king cake handy. "We take finding the baby seriously," Meshawn laughed. She said she loves the mystery of trying to figure out where it's hidden. "As a kid, I would just stare at the cake to see if there was a little bump giving it away!"

Growing up hasn't dampened the tradition. "Whoever gets the baby has to buy the next cake," she said. "And we're really competitive about that, too." Meshawn's brother likes Randazzo's king cakes best and tries to pressure whoever found the baby to bring one to the next party. But Meshawn doesn't succumb. She brings the cake she makes herself at Langenstein's, and though it might not satisfy her brother, everyone else is happy. "Oh my gosh, my kids love it when I bring king cake home from work. That's what the king cake tradition is to them."

Meshawn Gresham (center), Lakeya Simon (left), and Johana Moreno work in the bakery department at Langenstein's. During Carnival season they make as many as one hundred and fifty king cakes each day. Meshawn is holding their wedding cake king cake, Lakeya has a traditional king cake, and Johana is holding "The Screwball" king cake, made with Screwball Peanut Butter Whiskey.

Langenstein's, a small New Orleans-area grocery chain, is no stranger to making king cakes. A team of three or four work together to bake anywhere from sixty to one hundred and fifty king cakes each day, including a rotation of creative flavors. On the day of our photo shoot, Meshawn and her team made a traditional king cake, a wedding cake king cake filled with crumbled up wedding cake and Bavarian cream, and their "Screwball" king cake. The Screwball is filled and topped with Screwball Peanut Butter Whiskey, Bavarian cream, and crumbled Reese's Peanut Butter Cups.

The flavors are more creative than when Meshawn was a kid, but that's not all that is different. "Like most bakeries, we're not allowed to hide the baby in the cake anymore because of choking hazards and lawsuits," she said. But Meshawn and her family will usually hide it on their own. "One time we forgot to put it in, though, and my kids basically ate an entire cake looking for it!"

Some worry not including the baby inside the king cake might ruin an important Carnival tradition, but that's not what Meshawn has seen at her family gatherings or at Langenstein's. "Customers are always checking with us to make sure the baby's in the box, even if it's not in the cake," she said. "It's still a really important part of Carnival here, and I don't think it's going away, no matter where they put the baby."

LEFT PHOTOS: The Screwball king cake is filled with Bavarian cream mixed with Screwball Peanut Butter Whiskey. It's filled and topped with crumbled Reese's Peanut Butter Cups, and the topping also includes chocolate donut cake icing mixed with more peanut butter whiskey. **RIGHT PHOTOS:** The wedding cake king cake is filled with Bavarian cream and crumbled wedding cake. It's topped with chunks of wedding cake, icing, and almonds.

Hi-Do Bakery

"There are a lot of customers who love our king cake exactly because it doesn't have icing."

It's not uncommon, according to Kim Do, for a customer to walk into her parents' bakery during Carnival, see their king cakes have no icing and walk right back out the door. "But it's equally common," she said, "for customers to tell us this is their favorite king cake exactly *because* it doesn't have icing."

Today, icing is taken for granted by most New Orleanians as a king cake requirement. But until the 1970s, it was unheard of. For much of the twentieth century, the majority of New Orleanians ate exclusively McKenzie's king cakes. Those cakes weren't braided, didn't contain cinnamon, and definitely weren't iced. They were a bready brioche dough with purple, green, and gold sugar—light and fluffy, simple and delicious.

That's the kind of king cake Ha Do created after he first opened Hi-Do Bakery in 1989. "It fits our Vietnamese tastes," explained Kim. "We don't like things too sweet. The sugar on top is enough for us." The Dos aren't alone. For many New Orleanians at least thirty years old, this is one of the few king cakes remaining similar to what they loved growing up.

Hi-Do Bakery and their king cakes have been a family affair since 1991, when Kim, her siblings, and her mom, Huyen, were able to join Ha in America. But this was no easy reunion. They'd been separated for sixteen years, since Saigon fell to the Soviet Union-supported North Vietnamese. Ha was imprisoned after the war and escaped in 1981 to an Indonesian refugee camp. He made it to California three years later. After settling down in Louisiana and starting his bakery, he was finally granted permission to bring his family over.

During Carnival season, customers witness the whole family hard at work. "Not all of us work here year-round," Kim said, "but during Carnival, my parents, my sister, my brothers, my uncles, even my husband takes time off as a doctor to make king cakes. Sometimes we work until three in the morning, sleep two hours and are back at five."

LEFT PHOTO: Huyen (left) and Ha Do with their fleur de lis-shaped king cake. They offer a variety of special shapes also including a crab and a crawfish.

"We don't all work here year-round, but during Carnival, my parents, my sister, my brothers, my uncles, even my husband takes time off as a doctor to make king cakes."

That kind of labor is required during king cake season. "The investment it takes to maintain a bakery is huge," Kim said. "It's hot in Louisiana, and whole batches of bread can be ruined by temperature. It can lead to bankruptcy. Broken machinery can lead to bankruptcy, too. King cake gives us financial security."

It's taken decades for the Do family to find that security. They owe it to their perseverance and to their very popular king cake, but they also owe it to their loyal customers. Most mornings it's common to see Terrytown neighborhood regulars filing into Hi-Do for their favorite croissants and pastries. But come Mardi Gras season, customers come from across the region and beyond. "People who used to live here drive from hours away to taste the king cake they had as a kid," Kim said. Older generations tell her it's the closest thing to the McKenzie's cake taste they love so much. "But it's also the king cakes we love, so maybe we and New Orleans are just a really good match."

Icing wasn't popular on king cakes until the 1970s. Hi-Do king cakes still don't include it. They offer traditional king cakes with purple, green, and gold sugar, as well as football-themed king cakes with black and gold sugar.

Mae's Bakeshop

"Of course I care about the past. It helped make me who I am today."

For six years, Jeremy Fogg was the pastry chef at Emeril Lagasse's flagship restaurant, Emeril's. But he's dreamed of being a chef for far longer.

Jeremy's a nostalgic guy. "Of course I care about the past. It helped make me who I am today," he said. Many of Jeremy's best memories growing up in Orlando were of helping his grandmother prepare large family meals and decadent baked goods. To this day, he uses

baking recipes passed down from both of his grandmothers. He even has one-hundred-year-old recipes and equipment from his great-grandparents who were candymakers in North Carolina.

His first Carnival season as Emeril's pastry chef was in 2015. Despite only having lived in New Orleans for two years, it fell to Jeremy to create a signature king cake for one of the city's most respected restaurants. How did Jeremy respond? "I did what I often do when I'm challenged," he said. "I looked to my past."

Newcomers sometimes compare king cake to a Mardi Gras version of cinnamon buns, and Jeremy started with a similar thought. He used a family cinnamon roll recipe of his grandmother's sister-in-law. But Emeril's is a high-end restaurant. Jeremy knew he couldn't just dress a cinnamon roll in purple, green and gold. "Customers spend seventy-five dollars per person for a meal. I needed to elevate our king cake." Jeremy decided his cinnamon roll-flavored version would take the form of a pull-apart monkey bread. It was a cake he remembered from camping trips as a Boy Scout, and he thought diners would find it equally fun.

But Jeremy wasn't done elevating. To ensure the cake wasn't too dry, he researched a Japanese technique that allowed the dough to hold more water. To make sure his king cake wasn't too sweet, he used colorful Callebaut

OPPOSITE PAGE: Chef Jeremy Fogg's monkey bread king cake resting on a marble surface his great-grandparents used. They were candymakers in North Carolina.

> *"With New Orleans' culinary traditions, if you go into a restaurant and get jambalaya or collard greens, you know it's going to be the best jambalaya or collard greens you've ever had. I wanted that to be reflected in my king cake, as well."*

Crispearls™ instead of sugar. And rather than a plastic baby, he used a red bean—a localized ode to the thousands-year-old tradition of hiding a bean in the earliest iterations of king cake.

"With New Orleans' culinary traditions," he said, "if you go into a restaurant and get jambalaya or collard greens, you know it's going to be the best jambalaya or collard greens you've ever had. I wanted that to be reflected in my king cake, as well."

During the coronavirus pandemic, restaurants were shut down and Jeremy was unsure when he'd be able to return to work. He used the time to create his own bakery at home and Mae's Bakeshop was born. Mae is the middle name of both of Jeremy's grandmothers as well as his mother. "The name is my way of paying homage to the huge impact the women in my family have had on me," he said.

He's searching for a brick-and-mortar location, but until then Jeremy can be found at pop-ups and farmers markets around the city. His king cake was wildly popular last season and according to Jeremy, the best is yet to come. "Right now, I offer the one king cake with a Bananas Foster dipping sauce," he explained, "but when Mae's has a permanent home, I'll be able to offer some of my other favorites." That will include a sweet potato monkey bread king cake and a s'mores monkey bread variety. Each will have different dipping sauces to go with them.

Jeremy is someone who enjoys looking to the past. Still, he admitted, "There's a lot to look forward to, as well."

OPPOSITE PAGE: A piece of monkey bread king cake pulled apart and dipped into its accompanying Bananas Foster sauce.

Saba

"Just like New Orleanians argue over who has the best king cake, I've seen some heated debates among Jews over who's got the best babka!"

I n his 2018 cookbook, *Shaya: An Odyssey of Food, My Journey Back to Israel*, James Beard award-winning Chef Alon Shaya tells his story through recipes. The lutenitsa and lamb kebabs tell of his love for his Bulgarian-born grandparents, living far away in Israel where Alon was born. The red beans and rice and the ricotta cavatelli are love letters

to his adopted home of New Orleans and his passion for Italian cooking, respectively. The final chapter features recipes like matzo ball soup and baba ganoush, representing his reconnection with Judaism and his Israeli homeland.

For hundreds of years, king cake has been primarily associated with Catholics, so Alon's flagship restaurant, Saba, isn't where one would expect to find one of New Orleans' most yearned-after varieties. But maybe we shouldn't doubt him. While king cakes aren't common in the world's Jewish communities, Jews do have a

OPPOSITE PAGE: The babka king cake is topped with cinnamon streusel and drizzled with salted caramel. Miniature pomegranate figurines are used in place of the baby, a nod to Saba's restaurant group, Pomegranate Hospitality. In Judaism, the pomegranate symbolizes fertility and the renewal of life, much like the bean traditionally hidden in king cake. **TOP PHOTO:** James Beard award-winning Chef Alon Shaya (left) and Chef de Cuisine Copeland Crews with their popular king cake.

popular sweet, braided bread of their own.

It's called babka and, according to Copeland Crews, Saba's chef de cuisine, it shares a fun but challenging commonality with Louisiana's famous cake. "Just like New Orleanians argue over who has the best king cake," she said, "I've seen some heated debates among Jews over who's got the best babka!" At Saba, Alon, Copeland, and their team are making the case that the best of both breads might be under one roof.

They've created the babka king cake, and the first thing one notices is the way it looks. "The king cake shape is such a famous one," Copeland said, "but adding the babka texture and then slicing into it and seeing all the layers, it's a beautiful cake." Of course, it's the way the babka king cake tastes that is its major triumph. Babkas sometimes get a bad rap for being dry, but Saba solves that by soaking it in a cinnamon syrup. They add fresh orange zest as well as flakes of nutmeg you can see in the dough. But there's one ingredient Copeland

believes sets Saba's babka apart. "We whip in some olive oil, an ingredient in practically all our dishes," she said. "It's delicious, and it's also classic Saba."

The babka king cake is so popular the restaurant had to put a limit on the number they could make. "The poor woman who mixes the dough," Copeland laughed, "her arms nearly fell off!" To save limbs, increase production, and utilize freshly milled flour, the Saba team works with local Bellegarde Bakery to produce both king cakes and their famous pita. As a result, last year was the first time Saba was able to ship babka king cakes nationwide.

Copeland understands how passionate New Orleanians can be about their traditions, and she appreciates there's room for newer residents to mix a part of who they are into those customs. "Our king cake is Alon's story," she said. The story of an Israeli child who adored his grandparents and fell in love with New Orleans. It's all there in this special cake.

Viola's Heritage Breads

"Black people are behind some of the city's best food, but they don't get credit. We wanted to create a business in which people of color were acknowledged."

When Chef Carla Briggs and Kathryn Conyers founded Viola's Heritage Breads in March 2020, there were two motivations that drove them. The first was an immediate need. The coronavirus pandemic was spreading, disrupting supply chains, and leaving many grocery shelves empty. "You couldn't find a loaf of bread," Carla said. "And we thought, if big companies can't give our family, friends, and community the nutritious food they need, maybe we can."

The other motivation was a longer-term, institutional problem. "Black people are behind some of the best food in New Orleans," Carla explained. "Even if they're not the superstar chef, they're making the stock that makes that

Carla Briggs sits with her king cake in Congo Square. Long before European colonists arrived, Houma American Indians used the site for their harvest celebration. After becoming a French colony, enslaved Africans gathered here to make music, dance, and sell products.

chef's food so good. But they don't get credit. We wanted to create a business in which people of color were acknowledged."

Viola's Heritage Breads began with the bread Carla remembered her aunts and grandmothers making, recipes like tea cakes, honey butter cornbread, and more. As Carnival approached, Carla adapted a sweet potato rosemary bread, which had similar qualities to a brioche, to serve as the dough for her king cake. "King cake dough, especially when made from brioche, is so similar to bread, it felt natural to us," she said. "Plus, if you're a baker in New Orleans, how are you not going to make king cake?" Like a McKenzie's king cake, Carla's dough is bready, but Carla takes care to let you taste the butter and to add cinnamon and spice. She uses a sweet icing, more like a Randazzo's cake, but cuts that sweetness with citrus to complement the sweet potato.

When brainstorming locations for our photo shoot, Carla liked the idea of Congo Square. "I wanted to honor my ancestors and my city's heritage," she said. "So many creative people drummed, sang, danced, and sold their creations here, but we don't remember their names because they were enslaved."

Beginning in the eighteenth century, the French Code Noir required enslaved New Orleanians be given Sundays off. By 1817, Congo Square was the only place they were permitted to congregate. The result was hundreds, sometimes thousands, of Black residents gathering to make music and dance— gatherings many credit with the inventions of second lines and jazz. "What a lot of people don't realize is there was also a deep spirit of entrepreneurship here," explained Dr. Denise Graves of the Congo Square Preservation Society. "Enslaved craftsmen, clothing makers, and even bakers would sell their goods in Congo Square to earn revenue for themselves."

Carla is continuing that tradition of entrepreneurship, but she has no intention of remaining anonymous. In addition to baking bread that's wholesome and nutritious, she's gaining the skills necessary for mass production. "I want our bread to be on grocery shelves around the country," she said. "If you look at the companies already doing that, most don't value nutrition the way we do, and none of them are Black-owned. We'll change that."

TOP PHOTO: Carla (right) with Dr. Denise Graves of the Congo Square Preservation Society. Today, thanks in large part to the Society's work, New Orleanians continue to gather in Congo Square every Sunday afternoon to share their culture.

Chapter 3
FAMILY AND COMMUNITY

When I ate eighty-plus king cakes in 2017, I found myself frustrated that more bakeries didn't offer king cake by the slice. After expressing my annoyance at the financial strain of buying so many full-size cakes, my friend put me in my place. "Of course they don't sell slices," she said. "King cake is meant to be shared!"

She was right. During its three-century history in New Orleans, king cake has been a tradition enjoyed with others. When the cake first arrived here, it was eaten on Twelfth Night among Creole families. As the holiday became increasingly linked to Carnival and Mardi Gras in the nineteenth century, king cake was featured at more public gatherings like glamorous Carnival krewe balls. This introduced the cake to those outside Creole social circles. By the late-1800s, local newspapers reported on wealthy Anglo-Americans hosting "king cake parties" of their own. Things took another step at the turn of the century, when "return" king cake parties gained prominence, setting the expectation that the individual who found the cake's hidden favor would host the next party. It created a chain that could continue all season, guaranteeing social groups reconvened for several king cake parties throughout Carnival instead of only on Twelfth Night.

In the 1910s, king cake began to expand outside the city's socialite scene into individual homes. Bakers like Odenwald and Gros Caterers advertised, "A king cake will be a novelty at your table." Within decades, it would be a novelty no more. Thanks to increased advertising, teenagers soon caught the king cake bug, enjoying parties of their own by the 1940s. (Though it's said New Orleans parents begged their children not to eat a slice until the fève was already found for fear they'd be stuck hosting dozens of unruly children next week.)

Today, king cake is served at offices, classrooms, parties, and parades. Buying just a slice of king cake is the Carnival equivalent to playing catch with yourself. King cake is community, and in this chapter we'll look at bakeries that have made that community a central part of their business.

Dong Phuong Bakery

"It was a neighborhood of Vietnamese immigrants yearning for a taste of home. And my mom gave it to them."

Before they were honored with a James Beard Foundation award and before it was the norm to see hundreds of New Orleanians lined up outside their Dong Phuong Bakery in hopes of buying what's arguably the city's most popular king cake, Huong Tran, her husband De, and their children were refugees fleeing their war-torn Vietnam home. "We left hoping for opportunity, but we also left out of fear," explained Huong and De's daughter, Linh. De served in the Air Force for the American-backed South Vietnamese during the Vietnam War. When the North took over Saigon in 1975, he was imprisoned and then placed in a Communist "re-education camp."

But Huong and De met before all of that, teenagers in love. Huong worked at her parents' bakery and coffee shop, and De visited often. "My dad loved coffee," Linh laughed. "He drank it in place of water." When the war separated them, the two exchanged letters, dozens during the war and while De was imprisoned. And once he was released from the camp, he returned to Huong. They married and had two of their three children in Vietnam,

including Linh. They were attempting to start a new life. "But my parents were educated, and the communists were forcing everyone to become farmers," she said. "There was nothing for us there anymore, so we left."

It wasn't an easy journey. The young family left their possessions behind and had to bribe their way onto a boat carrying hundreds of passengers to Malaysia. Pirates boarded the boat and robbed them. Upon arriving, Malaysia wouldn't accept the refugees, saying the camp was full. But the desperate passengers wouldn't take no for an answer and Linh said her father jumped into the water and helped pull the ship ashore.

The Trans spent a year in the crowded refugee camp before learning De's best friend was sponsoring them to live with him in an American city called New Orleans. They arrived in 1979, but their journey was just beginning.

"My older brother and I were the first Vietnamese kids at our school," Linh remembered. "We were made fun of a lot at first." But they lived in the Versailles neighborhood of New Orleans East, a community growing with immigrants arriving from post-war Vietnam. De stocked groceries during the day and studied to become an engineer at night. Huong took the skills she'd learned at her parents' shop and made cakes and pastries to sell at local markets. "It was a neighborhood of Vietnamese immigrants yearning for a taste of home," Linh said. "And my mom gave it to them."

Seeing the businesses' potential, De left school and the family opened Dong Phuong Bakery in 1982. Since then, it's grown to unimaginable levels. Today, Dong Phuong sells nearly five thousand loaves of bread per day.

OPPOSITE PAGE: Dong Phuong founder Huong Tran stands with her coveted king cake in front of trays of her famous bread. Daily, the bakery sells five thousand loaves of bread. During Carnival season, they also sell twelve hundred king cakes each day.

Their brioche buns and pistolettes can be found in restaurants across the city.

But the climb hasn't been without tragedy. De passed away in 2004, and Hurricane Katrina devastated the neighborhood the following year. But the Trans and the neighborhood persevered. Well organized, Versaille was one of the quickest communities to rebuild. And when Dong Phuong got back on its feet, its biggest hit would soon follow.

"As a new generation of Vietnamese-Americans grew up in Versaille, they were much more attuned to what was going on in the rest of New Orleans," Linh explained. "During Carnival, that included king cake, and we wanted our customers to be able to get one here in the neighborhood." The family designed a cake to fit their community's taste, using the same buttery brioche dough already in many of Dong Phuong's most popular products. And instead of traditional sugar icing, they use cream cheese. "Our customers don't want something super sweet. The cream cheese makes it a little more savory."

Dong Phuong produces a mind-blowing twelve hundred king cakes daily, baking twenty-four hours per day for six days a week during Carnival season. Despite the massive number of cakes, they sell so fast that getting one can feel like discovering Willy Wonka's golden ticket in your chocolate bar. Except most New Orleanians would rather have the Dong Phuong king cake. "It makes me feel so proud," Linh said, "we were just a small family of refugees when we got here."

Four decades later, they're the new face of New Orleans king cakes.

PREVIOUS PAGE: When the Trans first moved to New Orleans, Huong sewed for neighbors as a source of income. This experience helped create the Dong Phuong king cake's unique shape. Huong wanted to make the traditional, round shape without braiding or breaking the dough. She remembered from sewing that if you want to make fabric bend, you make many little slits. This applies to dough as well (center photo) and gives the cake its signature scalloped edges.

Caywood & Randazzo's Bakery

"When people try ours and say it tastes like what grandpa and his dad and brothers used to make, it's an honor, because that's what a New Orleans king cake is to so many people."

There's no name in New Orleans today more closely associated with king cake than Randazzo. That connection began on April 1, 1965, when Sam Randazzo opened Hi-Lan Bakery just outside New Orleans in St. Bernard Parish with his three sons Lawrence, Anthony, and Manuel. In the nearly sixty years since, this original Randazzo clan sired and trained new Randazzo children and in-laws, many of whom started bakeries of their own. But these aren't collaborating franchises under a single banner. This is a story involving lawsuits, feuds, and good old-fashioned competition to see which Randazzo's king cake reigns supreme.

Beginning in the 1990s, two of Manuel's children, Manny, Jr. and Tricia, each opened bakeries of their own. Meanwhile, Lawrence's three children, Sal, Petrina, and Joel opened one together. When their bakery was destroyed by Hurricane Katrina, Joel and her husband, Felix founded another. Even divorce expanded the Randazzo reach, though a judge ruled that bakery had to go by a different name.

The most recent Randazzo's business to join the scene was Caywood & Randazzo's in

LEFT PHOTO: A baker braids the king cake dough before it's baked. **RIGHT PHOTO:** A unique aspect of all Randazzo's king cakes is that the colored sugar is added to the dough before it's baked. After coming out of the oven, the icing is added. Most Randazzo's bakeries top the icing with sprinkles, as pictured here. (Nonna Randazzo's uses nonpareils instead.)

2015, just two towns over from the original Hi-Lan Bakery. The shop was opened by another of Manuel's children, Susan, her ex-husband Kenneth Caywood, Sr., and their children Kenny, Jr. and Nick.

"We're not really interested in all the feuding and competition," explained Nick, one of several fourth-generation bakers across various lines of the Randazzo family. "We think ours is the best, but each Randazzo family bakery is basically using the same recipe." Nick said everyone at Caywood's learned to make king cake from his grandfather, Manuel. "When people try ours and say it tastes like what grandpa and his dad and brothers used to make, it's an honor, because that's what a New Orleans king cake is to so many people."

Kenneth, Sr. agreed keeping the old recipe is a point of pride. "We don't need gimmicks here," he said. "People love boudin king cakes and Chantilly king cakes, and Dong Phuong and their croissant dough gets lines out their door. But to us, what we make is the real king cake." And judging by how many they sell from their shop, the King Cake Hub, and other vendors around the region, there are a lot of Louisianians who agree. "That's the dream," Kenneth laughed, "work your butt off selling king cakes during Carnival, and then go fishing the rest of the year. Mission accomplished."

Members of the Caywood & Randazzo's team, including co-owners Kenneth Caywood, Sr. (left), Kenny Caywood, Jr. (center), and Nick Caywood (second from right). Kenny and Nick's mother is Susan Randazzo, daughter of Manuel Randazzo, one of the owners of the Randazzo family's original Hi-Lan bakery.

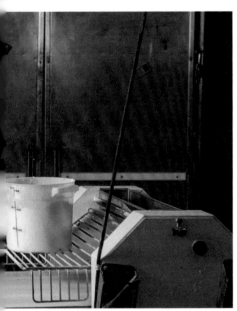

The Randazzo's King Cake Family Tree

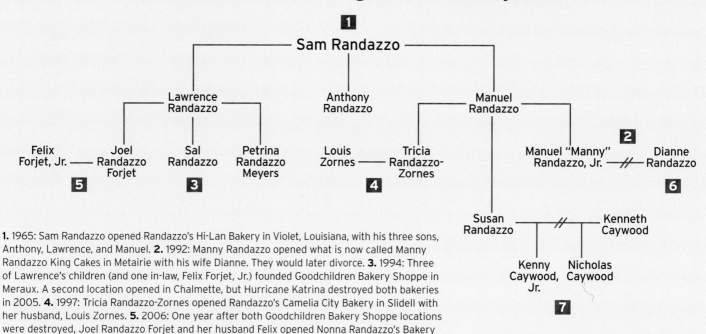

1. 1965: Sam Randazzo opened Randazzo's Hi-Lan Bakery in Violet, Louisiana, with his three sons, Anthony, Lawrence, and Manuel. **2.** 1992: Manny Randazzo opened what is now called Manny Randazzo King Cakes in Metairie with his wife Dianne. They would later divorce. **3.** 1994: Three of Lawrence's children (and one in-law, Felix Forjet, Jr.) founded Goodchildren Bakery Shoppe in Meraux. A second location opened in Chalmette, but Hurricane Katrina destroyed both bakeries in 2005. **4.** 1997: Tricia Randazzo-Zornes opened Randazzo's Camelia City Bakery in Slidell with her husband, Louis Zornes. **5.** 2006: One year after both Goodchildren Bakery Shoppe locations were destroyed, Joel Randazzo Forjet and her husband Felix opened Nonna Randazzo's Bakery in Covington. Additional locations would follow in Chalmette and Mandeville. **6.** 2008: After her divorce with Manny, Dianne founded a bakery, Dianne Randazzo LLC. The courts ruled she couldn't use the Randazzo name for her king cakes, so the business took on business partner John Caluda's name instead. Caluda's King Cake in Harahan makes a cake similar in some ways to a Randazzo's king cake, but nowhere near identical. **7.** 2015: Kenny and Nicholas Caywood opened Caywood & Randazzo's Bakery in Chalmette in 2015 with mother Susan and father Kenneth.

Norma's Sweets Bakery

"It's nice to see people from your adopted home appreciate what you've added to their tradition."

More than one hundred thousand Hondurans live in metro New Orleans, making it the largest such community in the country. They began immigrating to NOLA en masse in the 1960s, escaping floods, fruit company strikes, and military coups. Major companies producing bananas in Honduras were headquartered in New Orleans, creating an attractive destination for the refugees. But Jose Castillo, who moved here with his parents in 1980, believes New

Orleans benefited, too. "When different people come together and share their experiences, creativity doesn't have limits," he said. King cake is just one of many ways that creativity was realized.

Jose is the owner of Norma's Sweets Bakery in Mid-City, but his mother, the shop's namesake, still runs the original bakery in Kenner. It was never their plan to make king cakes, but Latin American customers began asking for them, especially as king cakes became more popular in the years following Hurricane Katrina. "I think they trusted my mom to make something that matched Latin American tastes better than what was already out there."

Norma created a guava cream cheese king cake, a popular flavor combination in Latin

Jose Castillo (third from right) and the Norma's Sweets Bakery team with their guava cream cheese king cake.

103

countries. But it wasn't just Latin Americans who loved it. "All sorts of New Orleanians gave us positive feedback," he said. "It's nice to see people from your adopted home appreciate what you've added to their tradition."

Jose said he loves how creative bakers have become with king cake, particularly among the city's different ethnic groups. As long as it tastes good, he said, the more options the better. "When I was young, all anyone talked about was McKenzie's. Now you have people coming from all over the world making new styles. Who would have thought a Honduran family could make a New Orleans king cake people loved?"

The Baby

Hiding a baby figurine in the Louisiana king cake is a tradition some believe began in the 1930s. Back then, McKenzie's Pastry Shoppes President Donald Entringer hid a bean in each of the approximately dozen king cakes he sold annually, but customers sometimes ate the bean instead of buying another cake as custom dictated. "We needed to come up with something that couldn't be eaten," Entringer told *The Times-Picayune* in a 1990 interview. One day a traveling salesman visited the bakery with a large supply of porcelain dolls we nowadays refer to as Frozen Charlottes, china dolls, kewpie dolls, penny dolls, or bisque dolls, and Entringer began hiding those inside his king cakes.

But McKenzie's wasn't the first to use the figurines. Frozen Charlottes (though they weren't called this in New Orleans until generations later) became popular thanks to an 1843 poem about a girl who froze to death after ignoring her mother's pleas to wear a coat. Between 1850 and 1920, miniature ceramic dolls sometimes appeared as a prize in birthday cakes. In New Orleans, the leap from birthday cake to king cake was natural.

One girl recorded in her 1899 diary, "It being 'King's Day' we ate some King's Cake, and my cousins and one of my aunts got the seeds, or as I had better say, the pecans and dolls as two had dolls." *The Daily Picayune* first mentioned a king cake baby in January 1908, reporting, "the king cake was cut, and the doll fell to Miss A. Barrow."

The king cake baby doesn't appear to have fully entered the city's lexicon until the 1940s. A 1947 ad from Picou's Bakery mentions their king cake contains a "traditional doll" while a McKenzie's advertisement from 1952 promotes their "China Doll." During the 1950s and '60s, Entringer engaged in an aggressive advertising campaign to popularize the baby, and it worked. He switched to cheaper, pink plastic figurines and other bakeries followed. Soon, nearly every king cake in the city had a baby hidden inside.

"I've heard people say it's supposed to represent the Christ Child, but that's not true," Entringer told *The Times-Picayune* when asked about the heated local debate over whether the baby's symbology is religious. "Why we picked this, I don't know, it was cute." Adding to the confusion, the baby figurine hidden in the Mexican rosca de reyes actually does represent Jesus. Could the earliest use of the baby in Louisiana cakes be connected to this custom without Entringer knowing?

The tradition has continued to change through the years. Beginning in the 1990s, a baby with brown "skin" was sometimes used (as were purple, green, and gold babies). Additionally, most bakers now leave hiding the baby to the customer for fear of liability if someone chokes, though a few local bakeries still hide the figurine themselves.

Gracious Bakery

"Let everyone bring in their own unique voice. That's what New Orleans and Mardi Gras are all about."

Gracious Bakery is one of this city's most beloved spots for baked goods. Much of that success is due to the skill of co-owner and New Orleans native Megan Forman. After graduating from the New England Culinary Institute, she worked in the award-winning pastry program at the Park Avenue Café in New York. She returned home to become pastry chef at Bayona and later helped start local sweets spot, Sucré. Ten years ago, she opened Gracious with her husband Jay and quickly saw how tight the profit margins of a bakery can be. "The summers are so slow here," she said, "you need something to push you through or you can't survive."

That something turned out to be king cakes. At first, Megan was resistant. As a kid, she wasn't a big

BOTTOM PHOTO: Gracious Bakery sells a "New Orleans King Cake Kit" so customers can enjoy making their own king cake at home. **RIGHT PHOTO:** A variety of Gracious Bakery king cake slices. Megan Forman's team features a rotating offering of Louisiana-style king cakes and galettes des rois each year.

fan of the ubiquitous McKenzie's cakes, saying they were too dry. As an adult, she felt modern versions were too sweet. But a baker in New Orleans really has no choice but to offer king cakes, she said. "A good Mardi Gras can help you get through the year, so I relented, and it's been really good for us."

Megan takes pride in creating king cakes that aren't overly sweet, and she isn't shy about experimenting with new flavors. In addition to a chocolate king cake, and a queen cake with almond frangipane, Gracious Bakery has offered varieties like cherries jubilee, Bananas Foster, satsuma, pretzel Nutella®, and even MoonPie. "I thought the MoonPie king cake was going to put my name in lights," she joked. But ultimately, it was a nectar cream king cake that caught fire. It has almond, cream cheese, and a nectar cream snowball syrup. "I think it's the nostalgic snowball flavor that people loved," she said. "Our plan was to do it for just one season, but when we didn't have it the next year, boy did we hear it!"

Because of the importance bakeries place on king cake season, the stage is set for intense competition for customers. But Megan doesn't see it that way. "Some people say ours isn't king cake because we don't braid our dough, but I don't understand that kind of exclusion," she said. "Let everyone bring in their own unique voice. That's what New Orleans and Mardi Gras are all about."

Megan is a huge fan of what new bakers are doing with their king cakes and tries her best to support them. "Have you had a king cake from S.S. Sweets?" she asked. "They're wonderful." Megan said rather than competing, collaboration is what's in the best interest of the city's bakeries. "When king cakes are doing well in this city, we're all doing well," she insisted. "It takes more than one cake to host a king cake party, right?"

Top-left, Bananas Foster king cake (left) and nectar cream king cake; top-right, king cake filled with chocolate (left) and almond frangipane-filled "Queen Cake;" bottom-right, two galettes des rois (one with Valrhona chocolate and cherry galette filling); bottom-left, a pair of Bananas Foster king cake slices.

Rouses Markets

"No matter what slice you get, or what cake you get, or what store you get it from, you're guaranteed to taste that cinnamon, Mardi Gras flavor!"

During the final week of Carnival, the St. Charles Avenue parade route stretches for miles with colorful beads flying from elaborately decorated, multi-tiered parade floats. A wall of sound emanates from the horns of hundred-person marching bands, and costumed revelers cheer them on beside tables full of beer, fried chicken, and, of course, king cake. More often than not, that king cake seems to be from Rouses Markets. But just how ubiquitous is the supermarket chain's popular cake? Let's look at the data.

In 2019, the New Orleans Metropolitan Convention and Visitors Bureau estimated at least seven hundred and fifty thousand king cakes are sold in New Orleans annually. Rouses Markets said, on their own, they sell a mind-melting five hundred thousand in that same time frame! Now, granted, Rouses' king cakes are baked fresh at each of their seventy-six supermarkets spread across three states, so all those king cakes aren't sold in New Orleans, but still, that's a lot of plastic babies! It's no wonder it feels nearly impossible to find a New Orleanian who hasn't tried one. But what makes it so popular?

"Customers are drawn to the same delicious

Rouses Markets has been making king cake since approximately 1970. Known for its agreeable price point and generous use of cinnamon, it's become one of the most widely eaten in New Orleans.

recipe we've used for years," explained Michelle Knight, Rouses' bakery director. That recipe starts with a sweet dough, which sits on the sweetness spectrum somewhere between the other two popular king cake dough options: a lightly sweetened, traditional brioche on one end; and a sweeter cinnamon roll dough on the other. Rouses' king cakes are also known for their affordability and their generous use of cinnamon. Rather than cinnamon powder, Michelle rolls a cinnamon sugar smear between each layer of dough. "No matter what slice you get, or what cake you get, or what store you get it from, you're guaranteed to taste that cinnamon, Mardi Gras flavor!"

As much as Michelle loves the taste of her king cake, it's the atmosphere around it she enjoys most. "The look on people's faces when you walk into a party, or onto the parade route, with a king cake is magic," she said. "That a cake I created can make so many people so happy is why I love being a baker."

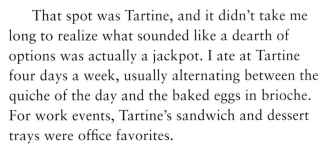

Tartine

"It's just a delicious, brioche dough rolled with cream cheese and cinnamon. Like everything else they make, it's nothing fancy. It's just extraordinary."

Tartine is the first New Orleans restaurant I fell in love with.

It was back in 2010 and I was starting a new job in the Black Pearl neighborhood. "As far as lunch, we have a great farmers market in the parking lot on Tuesdays," said my new boss, orienting me on the most pressing aspects of the job. "But other than that, there's only one spot within walking distance. It just opened."

That spot was Tartine, and it didn't take me long to realize what sounded like a dearth of options was actually a jackpot. I ate at Tartine four days a week, usually alternating between the quiche of the day and the baked eggs in brioche. For work events, Tartine's sandwich and dessert trays were office favorites.

And we weren't alone. Ray Cannata, the star of the 2012 documentary, *The Man Who Ate New Orleans*, agreed. "The food, like most everything at Tartine, isn't about going over the top," he explained. "They take fairly standard flavors, and they just make it better than other places. I don't know how Cara does it, but it's a triumph."

Cara is Cara Benson. That triumph is in large part due to the skill of her and her husband, Evan. They met at the prestigious French Culinary Institute in New York City before moving back to New Orleans. "New Orleans is where I learned to love food," she explained. Cara remembered her grandmother serving baguettes with jam, cheese, and cured meats when she was a child. A young Cara baked cakes and pastries and delighted in playing with cookbooks to try new recipes. "I've always loved the effect food has on people. That's the reason I went down this path. Food makes people happy, and I like being a part of that."

One visit to Tartine and it's obvious how happy her cafe makes her customers. The only thing keeping Tartine at least somewhat a secret is its location in a far-off corner of the city, nestled near the river where Uptown approaches the Jefferson Parish border. Ray said he's thankful Tartine has kept some anonymity, otherwise, come Carnival season, he'd have a tougher time getting his favorite king cake.

LEFT PHOTO: Cara Benson with her king cake in front of her bakery, Tartine. It's been a Black Pearl neighborhood favorite since opening in 2010.

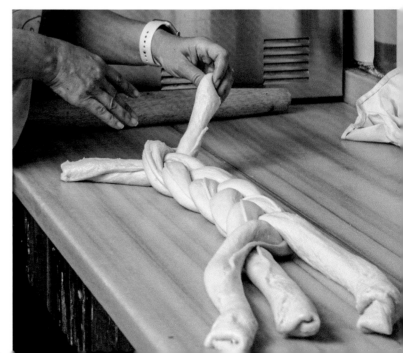

"It's just a delicious, brioche dough rolled with cream cheese and cinnamon. Like everything else they make, it's nothing fancy. It's just extraordinary."

But achieving the perfect king cake takes time. Cara said her first cakes were drier than she would have liked, and they sometimes had undesirable air gaps. Fixing the kinks required experimenting with different temperatures and baking times, as well as tweaking the amounts of icing, filling, and brioche. Today, someone who orders a king cake from Tartine—or from one of its three sister restaurants, each named Toast—is guaranteed to consistently receive one that more than a few New Orleanians believe is the city's best.

One of my favorite things about Cara's king cakes is how some of the filling bursts through

OPPOSITE PAGE: Tartine's king cake is filled with cinnamon cream cheese.

the dough while baking. It turns golden brown in the oven, and it's a unique and delicious surprise when you bite what you think is dough, only to realize it's a baked piece of cinnamon cream cheese instead. "My husband calls those king cake cookies," Cara laughed. "It's his favorite part, too!"

Cara's favorite part of her king cake, on the other hand, is the joy it brings her neighbors and customers. It reminds her of what she loved about the season as a child. "My dad had an apartment on the corner of St. Charles and Washington avenues, and we wouldn't miss a parade. We'd have tons of friends and family over, red beans and etouffee on the stove, and a Party Palace king cake from Langenstein's on the counter," she remembered. "I treasure those memories, and if there are New Orleans kids today who have that memory with a Tartine king cake, then that's pretty special to me."

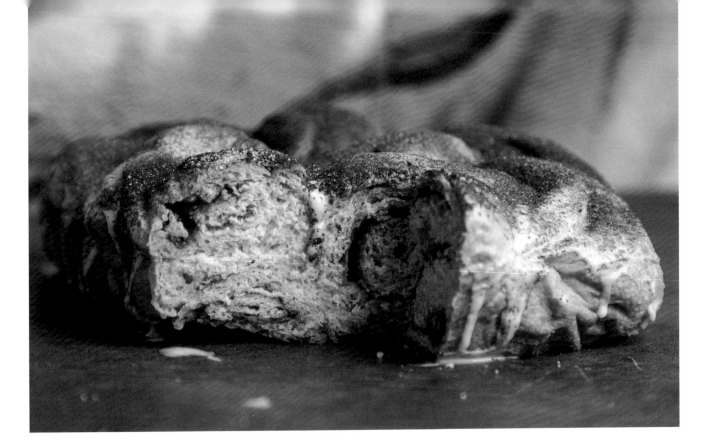

The Whiticar's Effect

"Honestly, it's what I love most about the business. Working with my mother is such a blessing."

The Whiticar family has no shortage of entrepreneurs. April Whiticar is the baker, her sister creates specialty drinks, and her mother, nicknamed "the Queen of Gumbo," focuses on soul food. Today, you can find them, along with April's father and grandmother, on their food truck, The Whiticar's Effect. And while things are looking up now, the family's faced their share of challenges.

Hurricane Katrina forced the Whiticars to uproot their lives and move to Houston. It wasn't until April's brother enrolled at LSU ten years later that some came back. April, however, decided to stay in Texas. "I have a family of my own in Dallas now," she said, "and my own business." That business is her bakery, Pearl's Sweet Creations, which specializes in, among other things, king cakes. "There's not a lot of king cakes in Dallas, so I jumped to fill that need."

When the coronavirus pandemic hit, April's mother, Karen, noticed people needed new ways to get food outside of restaurants. She applied for her LLC, found a truck, and called on her enterprising daughters. The Whiticar's Effect was born, and April travels to New Orleans at least five times a month to cook with

LEFT PHOTO: The Whiticar's Effect is staffed by April (left), Karen (right), Dorothy, and Matthew.

OPPOSITE PAGE, TOP PHOTO: A mini strawberry and whipped cream king cake (left) and a mini praline king cake. OPPOSITE PAGE, BOTTOM PHOTO: Two miniature crawfish king cakes topped with shredded cheddar and mozzarella cheeses and green onions.

her mother. "Honestly, it's what I love most about the business," she said. "Working with my mother is such a blessing."

The truck specializes in soul food like bell pepper and Philly cheesesteak rolls. Come Carnival, however, they also sell a variety of April's king cakes ranging from traditional, to filled, to savory.

April's grandmother, Dorothy, is an entrepreneur in her own right, starting a hair salon, a real estate business, and even buying a strip mall so other enterprising family members could open businesses of their own. When she sees The Whiticar's Effect, she said, she beams with pride. "I was always taught to be a leader and not to wait for others to give you an opportunity," Dorothy said. "You work hard, and you do something for your community. And when I watch April with her bakery, and her and her mom with this truck, and so many other members of my family, I can see the lessons I was taught passed down to them."

The Sweet Life Bakery

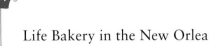

"I learned quickly that when the Saints are doing well, people buy three times as many king cakes and they want black-and -gold everything."

"There's no doubt in my mind, Drew Brees 100 percent affects king cake sales," Jenny Pacaccio declared as she shook golden sugar onto a cookie butter-filled king cake.

Before dismissing her theory, it's important to establish Jenny knows a thing or two about selling food. In addition to founding The Sweet Life Bakery in the New Orleans suburb of Metairie, her parents owned the beloved Carmine's Italian & Seafood Grill.

Her experience with how the legendary New Orleans Saints quarterback can lift or tank king cake consumption began in January 2010. Jenny had just opened her bakery as the Saints were knocking off playoff opponents on their way to a Super Bowl. "I learned quickly that when the Saints are doing well, people buy three times as many king cakes and they want black-and-gold everything," she said. "We made Saints-colored king cakes and they sold like crazy."

Jenny's king cakes are a compromise between her tastes and those of her customers. "My grandma was a huge McKenzie's fan," Jenny recalled. "Their king cake was her favorite." McKenzie's king cakes were developed in the 1930s and 1940s, decades before icing became popular. Famously, a McKenzie's king cake only had the purple, green, and gold sanding sugar on it. When Jenny first created her king cakes, she followed McKenzie's lead. Not all her customers were happy. "I got so much resistance at first. Some people wanted icing on it because they like a very sweet dessert," she said. "That's not my preference. I want to taste that cookie butter filling, for example, not just frosting." The compromise was to add an icing barely thicker than donut glaze, but far thinner than the

LEFT PHOTO: Bakery owner Jenny Pacaccio with her king cake. Her shop is decorated with Krewe of House Float-style flowers from the coronavirus-impacted 2020 Carnival season. The flowers were created by local artists at Stronghold Studios.

heftier, sometimes even whipped, icing found on many other king cakes.

The solution was well received. King cake sales have generally increased over the last several years. Jenny hopes that trend will continue, but this year, she notes, there's one key difference. "Drew Brees is retired now, so I don't know if the Saints will be good," Jenny said, "and if the Saints aren't good, they won't be playing football come Carnival season." No playoff football means no king cakes for playoff football watch parties. But Jenny's hopeful that even in the unthinkable situation that the Who Dats don't make the playoffs, New Orleanians will find a reason to gather and eat king cake.

"Last June my ten-year-old daughter asked me, 'Now that crawfish season is over, how are we going to get together with everyone?' I told her we've got barbecues next, then Saints games, then the holidays, then king cake parties. We're always gathering for something in New Orleans and come Carnival season, those gatherings always have a king cake— usually many!"

LEFT PHOTO: A slice of cookie butter-filled king cake (left) beside an almond frangipane-filled slice.

Joe's Café

"I know everyone says they have the best king cakes, but we really do have the best."

Joe's Café is named for the everyman, the average Joe, the kind of person who enjoys a cup of joe. And that's evident when you look around the cafe. Older couples and friends sit at tables with a glazed donut, a coffee, and a newspaper. Middle-aged men and women rush in and quickly leave with a dozen donuts for their office or their kid's school.

To Justin Armand, who co-owns the seven Joe's Cafés in the New Orleans area with his dad,

James, these diner-esque donut shops have been a huge part of his life. His dad opened the first one in 1988 when Justin was just a year old. His earliest memories are of sitting on a donut table while his dad cut donuts and made king cakes. Justin's only job back then was to eat the baked goods, the same job his three kids have today. "They love it here," he laughed. "I mean, what kid isn't going to like hanging out at a donut shop? Maybe they'll work here one day, too."

If they do, Justin and James will be able to use the help. Especially during Carnival season, when they make and sell as many as seven thousand king cakes. Just like their donuts, they feature a lot of different varieties including strawberry cream cheese and pecan praline. But just as their basic glazed donuts outsell the adventurous ones, traditional king cakes sell best.

"People say the old traditional king cakes didn't use cinnamon," Justin explained, "but cinnamon is such an integral part of traditional king cakes nowadays. And it's something I really love about our cakes."

Justin's loved these cakes since he was a child. He remembered being in school during Carnival and each week a different student would be responsible for bringing in the king cake. Everyone else would bring in what Justin described as "basic king cakes," but when it was Justin's turn, he brought in his dad's.

"I know everyone says they have the best king cakes," he said, pausing with a smile. "But we really do have the best. I was a popular kid any day I brought dad's king cakes into school."

LEFT PHOTO: Justin Armand with his pecan praline and strawberry cream cheese king cakes.

Levee Baking Co.

"Things have really changed in the last fifteen years. People value the local, intimate, and unique more than they have in generations."

Something that sets Levee Baking Co. apart is owner Christina Balzebre's dedication to all things local. That dedication begins with a love for New Orleans, the city Christina's called home for sixteen years. "After graduating from Loyola University, I wanted two things," she said. "To stay in New Orleans and to work literally any job in a kitchen." And over the years, Christina worked just about all of them, serving as a dishwasher, juicer, line cook, prep cook, sandwich maker, and bread baker.

Each of those jobs nudged Christina toward the baker she is today. During three years at Satsuma Café, for example, she gained experience building relationships with local farmers. "By the time I started doing my first pop-ups for Levee Baking," she said, "I was committed to sourcing as many local ingredients as possible." That's evident in her king cake, a traditional French galette des rois. "The paste inside is typically almond," Christina explained, "but why not use local pecans instead?" She also adds a citrus element to her galettes. Rather than committing to one fruit all season, she purchases what's available locally each week.

Christina fosters local collaborations as well. Before opening her permanent location, she was invited by Uptown restaurant Mosquito Supper Club to share kitchen space. This led to a partnership with ceramist Jackie Brown, who also had a studio there. One of Jackie's ongoing projects was creating porcelain fèves that were traditionally hidden inside king cakes, particularly in France. Jackie began that work when a neighbor found an old fève in the shape of a person buried in their backyard and gave it to her. Jackie made a mold so she could create

LEFT PHOTO: Levee Baking Co. owner Christina Balzebre with her galette des rois. The galette is traditionally filled with an almond paste, but Christina uses local ingredients like pecans instead. **OPPOSITE PAGE, BOTTOM PHOTO:** Each galette comes with a fève created by local ceramicist Jackie Brown. Fèves are commonly found in the galette des rois in France.

more and began selling them to hobbyists and collectors. "I saw them at our shared space and was obsessed," Christina said. "I thought they'd be perfect in my galette, just like the French do."

The partnership started off small in 2018, with Christina ordering about ten fèves at a time. Last year, however, as word of Levee Baking's excellence spread, Christina ordered more than four hundred to keep up with the rising volume of king cake orders.

Christina believes the local, handcrafted nature of her king cake has helped them standout. "Things have really changed in the last fifteen years," she said. "People value the local, intimate, and unique more than they have in generations. Whether it's the ingredients, Jackie's fèves, or just recognizing me and my staff at our bakery, I think people want to feel connected to the products they buy. Ours are about as local as you can get."

The Fève

The word fève translates from French to broad bean, favor, or charm. This includes anything hidden in a king cake granting royalty or predicting good fortune.

Beans have served the role of fève since the ancient Romans. By the time Christianity commandeered the tradition for Epiphany in the late Middle Ages, the bean exhibited an unexpected weakness. Then, the tradition sometimes required the newly crowned king to pay for everyone else's drinks. To avoid footing the bill, legend has it some would simply swallow the bean before anyone knew they'd found it.

Whether it was to thwart our ancestral cheapskates, or it was part of the Church's plan to

swap out pagan symbols for Christian ones, the bean was replaced by a beautifully decorated—and hard to swallow—porcelain fève, commonly a crown to commemorate those Three Kings who found the baby Jesus.

But the crown fève ran into trouble during the late-eighteenth century, namely the French Revolution. The victorious revolutionaries attempted to wipe out all symbolism related to the monarchy. Not just the crown fève, but also the king cake itself, faced the guillotine.

Both survived, but over the next two-and-a-half centuries, the French considered new options for what could be depicted as fève. Movie stars, works of art, cartoon characters, and even the 2018 World Cup champion men's soccer team have all been represented in terracotta form. The country's top pastry chefs command designer fèves such as limited-edition puzzle pieces to be assembled, or a series of ceramic Kama Sutra positions. Each year, "fabophiles," as they're called, meet in Paris for an international fève fair to buy, sell, and swap their favorites.

And it's not just the French. Countries around the world use coins, beans, figurines, and even fortunes in their versions of king cake. In nineteenth century New Orleans, beans or pecans were most common. Today, of course, the plastic baby reigns supreme, but local bakeries such as Levee Baking Co., Celtica Bakery, and Haydel's Bakery offer beautifully decorated annual fèves that allow interested Louisianians to become fabophiles, as well.

La Boulangerie

"There's this six-to-eight-week period where New Orleanians' eyes are on bakers and pastry chefs. That doesn't happen in other places!"

Pastry chef Maggie Scales still can't believe the attention her industry gets during Carnival season. "There's this six-to-eight-week period where New Orleanians' eyes are on bakers and pastry chefs," she said. "That doesn't happen in other places!"

Originally from Philadelphia, Maggie didn't realize what she was getting into as her first Twelfth Night approached. It was 2011, and she was pastry chef at the French Quarter's Omni Royal Hotel. She'd just successfully navigated a busy Thanksgiving, Christmas, and New Year's,

and was ready for a break. "My sous chef said, 'Break?! What are you talking about? It's about to get crazier.'" He asked what kind of king cake Maggie was planning, and when she admitted she had no idea what he was talking about, they knew she had to learn fast.

The sous chef brought in ten king cakes from around the city to kickstart Maggie's education. "I couldn't believe how many different styles and cakes there were, even in that small sampling," she said, "but it helped me figure out what I liked and what I didn't." Maggie wasn't a fan of the heavy, unsweetened brioche dough common in Louisiana king cakes during the middle of the twentieth century. Her preference was a sweet, cinnamon roll-type Danish dough. "Randazzo's became my model early on."

TOP-LEFT PHOTO: Pastry chef Maggie Scales with her traditional king cake from La Boulangerie. **OPPOSITE PAGE:** In place of a plastic baby, Maggie's king cakes are served with a pig figurine because of the bakery's connection to Donald Link's restaurant, Cochon.

Two years later, Maggie was pastry chef at La Boulangerie, owned by Donald Link. One year after, she was the executive pastry chef overseeing all six of his restaurants, including the production of a wildly popular galette des rois from La Boulangerie and the creative "Elvis" king cake from Cochon Butcher. But just because she inherited these king cakes doesn't mean she stopped working to improve them or recipes for the new king cakes she was creating. Whether adding potato flour to make a softer, longer-lasting dough, or working to create cake that was lighter and sweeter, Maggie was always perfecting.

After eight years of king cake-making, this is the first season Maggie feels she won't need to adjust her recipe. That doesn't mean she's done learning. Nearly every day during Carnival season, someone from the La Boulangerie team brings in another bakery's king cake to try. "It's not some competitive spying thing," Maggie said. Instead, it's an opportunity to celebrate the local baking community's talent and creativity. "Though, if I'm being honest, there have been a few times I'm like, 'Damn! Why didn't I think of that?!'"

But just because Maggie isn't in competition with other bakers doesn't mean a heated king cake rivalry doesn't exist among the city's residents. "It's crazy how hard people defend the king cake they think is best," she laughed. "That's not common in other cities. People passionately debating bakeries—as a baker, that's amazing to see."

La Boulangerie's French galette des rois has been one of the city's most popular for decades.

136

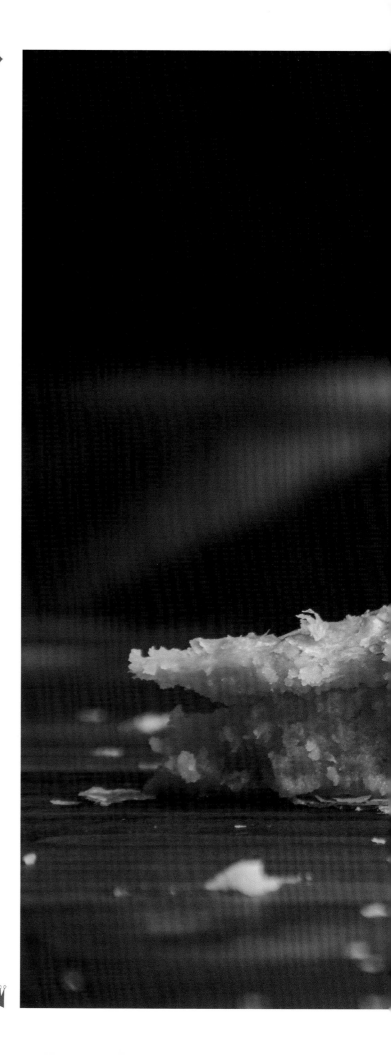

Chapter 4
DECADENCE

There's a reason Mardi Gras doesn't translate to "Slim Tuesday." In much the same way the ancient Romans celebrated Saturnalia, New Orleanians—already a rowdy bunch—enjoy Carnival season with copious amounts of alcohol, food, song, dance, and general merriment.

The season was designed to be decadent. Carnival comes from the Latin expression *carne vale*, which translates to "farewell to meat" or "farewell to flesh." Those farewells are because Mardi Gras—Carnival's final day—is on the eve of Lent. The Lenten season remembers Jesus' forty-day fast as many Christians make sacrifices of their own, abstaining from meat, dairy, fat, and sugar. It's billed as a time of voluntary deprivation. However, what if the origins of Lent aren't voluntary, but necessary? In early agrarian societies, late-February and early-March were historically difficult. The year's first crops were only starting to sprout while the meat, potatoes, and apples stored for winter flirted with spoilage. Rationing was required, and when entering a period of want, it's a good rule to get your fill beforehand. That's one of Carnival's original purposes: an opportunity to put on a few pounds before a period of scarcity.

Today, Catholic-dominated cultures around the world use Mardi Gras as an opportunity to rid their pantries of the fatty foods they'll attempt to avoid during Lent. In most places, it's some version of deep-fried dough. Italians have castagnole and cenci, Polish have pączki, Germans have fastnacht, Marylanders have kinkling, and the British and Irish eat pancakes with lemon juice and sugar. Russians have a butter festival and Icelanders call Fat Tuesday, *Sprengidagur*, which means "Bursting Day."

For generations of New Orleanians, it was the doughnut or beignet that was the local Mardi Gras indulgence while king cake was relegated to the backwaters of Twelfth Night. Today, king cake has taken over the season, and to say it's risen to the level of decadence is an understatement. In this chapter we'll look at varieties made of everything from Nutella® and cannoli cream to boudin and foie gras. Fat Tuesday, indeed.

Cochon Butcher

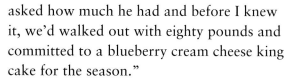

"Locally raised meat is better for the local economy, the animals are treated better, it's healthier for humans, and it's better for the planet. Plus, it just tastes better."

Under the leadership of Executive Pastry Chef Maggie Scales, the Link Restaurant Group's pastry department developed a reputation for using local ingredients to invent creative king cakes. At their Uptown bakery, La Boulangerie, for example, one of several king cakes they create each year is fruit-based, featuring produce from regional farmers. Strawberries are a common filling for Maggie as they're in season in Louisiana during Carnival, but she's tried other fruit, as well. "One year a Mississippi farmer had a surplus of blueberries frozen from the summer," she remembered. "I

asked how much he had and before I knew it, we'd walked out with eighty pounds and committed to a blueberry cream cheese king cake for the season."

However, La Boulangerie isn't the only eatery, or even the first, in the Link Restaurant Group to utilize local ingredients in their Carnival cakes. For nearly ten years, Cochon Butcher has served the "Elvis," a king cake filled with peanut butter and roasted banana, then topped with toasted marshmallow, Mardi Gras-colored sprinkles, and house-cured bacon. And this is no grocery store pork. Cochon Butcher breaks down about two thousand pounds of meat in-house each week from pigs raised in Mississippi and Louisiana. To Butcher General Manager Zack Shelton, using local meat makes a real difference. "It's better for the local economy, the animals are treated better, it's healthier for humans, and it's better for the planet," Zack said. "Plus, meat raised on local farms just tastes better. You can literally taste the difference."

The same can be said for the Elvis. There's no king cake in the city that tastes like it. Today we're used to the idea of eccentric king cakes, but that wasn't the case when Butcher revealed the Elvis a decade ago. "When it was first created," Zack said, "it was one of the city's craziest." The unique cake was invented when a former employee with the Link Restaurant Group realized rock legend Elvis Presley's birthday was on January 8, just two days after

OPPOSITE PAGE: Butcher Patrick Chauffe takes a bite of the Elvis king cake right off the cleaver. Don't try this at home.

Twelfth Night. "Elvis was known for living a decadent lifestyle," Zack explained, "and that included what he ate. His favorite sandwich was this crazy thing involving marshmallow fluff, peanut butter, bacon, and bananas." Cochon Butcher's next step seemed obvious: a creation that married Carnival, the birth of a rock legend, and their shop's spectacular local pork. To make their king cake stand out even more, instead of the traditional baby figurine, Butcher topped it

with a tiny plastic pig.

Those curious to try the Elvis can order it by the slice at Cochon Butcher during Carnival season, along with a slate of locally sourced meats and delicious sandwiches. If you want to buy a full king cake, it's best to call and order at least a day in advance. Zack said that customers begin calling about pre-orders weeks before Carnival season begins. "It might not be for everyone," he said, "but if you're an adventurous eater, you'll love it."

And Zack should know. "I've worked at Butcher for three years, and every day of Carnival I make sure to try at least a little piece."

To make sure the team is maintaining a high quality cake?

"Uh, yeah," he laughed, "sure, call it quality control. But let's just say it passes every time."

TOP PHOTOS: The marshmallow spread on top of the Elvis king cake is toasted before the locally sourced, house-cured bacon is added. **LEFT PHOTO:** Manager Jacques Couvillon (right) with Sassy, the Cochon Butcher mascot. **OPPOSITE PAGE:** Instead of a baby figurine, the Link Restaurant Group tops their king cakes with a tiny plastic pig, possibly related to Sassy.

Palm & Pine

"I don't know if there's a place in the world with a more indulgent nightlife and food scene than New Orleans, and in a lot of ways, king cake is the epitome of that."

"We weren't born in New Orleans, but we got here as fast as we could!" joked Amarys Herndon, who co-owns North Rampart Street restaurant, Palm & Pine with her husband Jordan.

There was a lot that drew the Herndons to the city more than a dozen years ago. But one thing they noticed immediately was its decadence. "I don't know if there's a place in the world with a more indulgent nightlife and food scene than New Orleans," Jordan said, "and in a lot of ways, king cake is the epitome of that."

That city-wide sense of hedonism inspired the recipe for Palm & Pine's unique and coveted king cake. "We figured, if we were going to create our own king cake, why not add the most decadent ingredient imaginable?"

That ingredient is foie gras —the fattened liver of a duck or goose, particularly popular in French cuisine. The Herndon's use foie gras in their king cake's filling, as well as in shaved form for its topping.

They debuted the cake in 2015, and it proved popular at Carnival season pop-ups around town. After they opened Palm & Pine in 2019, the king cake became a Mardi Gras hit at the restaurant, though elusive as they only make about twenty leading up to Fat Tuesday. That's by design, though, because despite how good their king cakes are, Palm & Pine is not a bakery. A restaurant first, they can't dedicate much effort to king cake without detracting from their regular menu.

BOTTOM-RIGHT PHOTO: Shaved foie gras tops each slice of Palm & Pine's king cake.

> ## "I think part of what makes king cake special is that you can't always get it. When you can, you've got to celebrate like you mean it."

"It feels like no matter how many we make, we're going to sell out," explained Amarys, "but I think part of what makes king cake special is that you can't always get it. When you can, you've got to celebrate like you mean it." Amarys said she associates king cake with Fat Tuesday—a table full of Zapp's, Zulu coconuts, some beers, and a half-eaten king cake. "That's not something you can do every day, but it's special when you can."

Palm & Pine occasionally has a whole king cake available for sale, but the best way to get your hands on the Herndon's foie gras cake is to make a reservation at the restaurant during Carnival. You can order a slice for dessert. And, like the best desserts, it's plenty decadent.

OPPOSITE PAGE: The decadent foie gras king cake is stuffed and topped with foie gras. Each slice even comes with a piece of foie gras on the side.

Bittersweet Confections

"If you love chocolate, then I think our king cakes are unbeatable."

Any New Orleans chocoholic worth their cacao knows about the chocolate king cakes at Bittersweet Confections. The original version has been around for quite some time—chocolate cream cheese baked into a brioche dough and covered with dark chocolate ganache. But, in case that's not enough chocolate for you, last year the bakery released the "Bittersweet King Cake." It's filled

with chocolate mousse, covered in that same dark chocolate ganache, and then topped with homemade chocolate truffles. If you're a fan of the old school sanding sugar-only king cakes, Bittersweet's are very different. "But if you love chocolate," said bakery founder Cheryl Scripter, "then I think our cakes are unbeatable."

There must be a lot of chocolate lovers in New Orleans, then. During Carnival season, Cheryl and her team make more than one thousand king cakes each week. It's difficult work, but Cheryl loves it. And that love can be traced all the way back to her childhood.

With the exception of the occasional trip to the neighborhood McKenzie's bakery, Cheryl's mother wouldn't let her and her sisters buy processed treats. "She told us if we wanted something sweet," Cheryl remembered, "then we had to bake it ourselves." Thanks to a family-wide sweet tooth, Cheryl and her sisters were up to the challenge. "I have so many great memories from that time. Fighting with my sisters over who would lick the bowl. Watching our dad try every cookie, brownie, and cupcake we made. It was magic."

As an adult, Cheryl eventually found her way back to that magic. She moved home to New Orleans in 1997 and slowly turned a passion for chocolate into a business, first selling chocolates from home, then at farmers markets, and finally at Bittersweet Confections, which she opened in

LEFT PHOTO: Cheryl Scripter with her "Bittersweet King Cake" topped with homemade chocolate truffles.
OPPOSITE PAGE: A slice of the "Bittersweet King Cake" with Bittersweet Confections' original chocolate king cake (left) and traditional king cake in the background.

"For those weeks, we're in king cake production twenty-four hours per day. It's truly chaos."

2013. Today, Cheryl owns two shops, and she sells everything from chocolate and coffee to sandwiches and, of course, king cake. Because of that king cake, Carnival is by far the craziest time of the year. "For those weeks, we're in king cake production twenty-four hours per day," she said. Thirty-thousand-dollar mixers are pushed to the limit. Coolers for dough are rolled out into the middle of the dining room. "It's truly chaos."

Cheryl wishes her parents could see the chaos. She wishes they could see how she made a career out of baking, how she still bakes and cooks with her children the way they used to with theirs, and how the family's sweet tooth lives on as they rush through Thanksgiving turkey to get to dessert. "I think they'd be proud," Cheryl said. "They'd love to see the impact they've had on our lives."

ABOVE: Cheryl prepares her "Bittersweet King Cake." **NEXT PAGE:** Top-left, original chocolate king cake; top-right, traditional king cake; bottom, the "Bittersweet King Cake."

Cakez & Cocktailz

"As adults or parents, we're always catering to someone else. I wanted to create a treat for grown-ups."

Nicole Johnson began baking sixteen years ago. "I just had my daughter and was spending a lot of time thinking, 'How are moms supposed to act?'" she explained. "I'd never done it before, you know? One conclusion I came to was I wanted to be a mom who could bake." That idea likely sprung from Nicole's own childhood when her mom would make her cookies. She thought they were good, but it was pre-made dough from the store. Nicole wanted to up her "mommy game." She dreamed of welcoming her daughter home from school with a plate of chocolate chip cookies made from scratch. "I liked the idea of her walking into the house to tastes and smells that were nostalgic, comfortable, and felt like home. Basically, I wanted to be the Black Martha Stewart!"

By her daughter's third birthday, Nicole was an accomplished cake maker and designer. "People saw the cake I made for her party and asked if I could make them one," she recalled. "Suddenly I was in business!" Over the years, her company grew and her skills increased. She accomplished her goal—baking for her daughter

and starting a business. But the profit margins for a home bakery are tight and Nicole sometimes only made enough to cover ingredient costs. Fortunately, her best idea was still to come.

"It all went back to being a single mom," Nicole said when asked how she came up with the idea for her boozy bakery Cakez & Cocktailz. "As adults or parents, we're always catering to someone else. I wanted to create a treat for the grown-ups." Nicole started by hosting parties where attendees could decorate cakes, sip wine, and relax with friends. Soon she sold her boozy desserts at pop-ups around New Orleans, including at the dog friendly, Marigny neighborhood bar Pepp's Pub.

During Carnival, customers asked Nicole to make adult king cakes, as well. Last year she taught herself how, modeling them after

OPPOSITE PAGE: Top, Hennessy pecan king cake; bottom, chocolate bourbon bacon king cake with drinks from Pepp's Pub. **RIGHT PHOTO:** Chef Nicole Johnson and four-legged companion Mija with a slice of Nicole's king cake.

her childhood favorites. "My mom loved McKenzie's, but I found them dry," she said. "For me, I loved king cakes like Antoine's and Randazzo's. They had the softer dough and put their 'fillings' in pockets on top like a Danish, instead of inside like a donut." Nicole uses a similar process with her king cakes, but that's where the commonalities end. "Other places already have the traditional flavors covered," she said, "so I cater to the adults."

Nicole ships her king cakes, as well, so adults near and far can enjoy varieties—with booze or without—like her Hennessy pecan king cake and her chocolate bourbon bacon king cake.

Twin's Burgers & Sweets

"He came in and whispered, 'Can we talk in the back? I've got an idea I think there might be some interest in,' which turned out to be an incredible understatement."

Western Louisiana is known for boudin, a local mixture of pork and rice inside a pork sausage casing. To say University of Louisiana at Lafayette Professor of History Dr. Bob Carriker is a fan is an understatement. Bob's nicknames include "Dr. Boudin" and "The Boudin King." He runs a website called BoudinLink.com, dedicated to the history and rating of boudin. He gives boudin tours throughout Cajun country, and he's the founder of the Boudin Cook-off, rated one of the top food festivals in America by *Gourmet Magazine.*

In his spare time, of which he can't have much, he enjoys cooking, often with, as you probably guessed, boudin. "I'll sometimes put the food I create on my website, and it'll get some attention," he said, "but when I posted photos of my boudin king cake in 2015, that response was on a completely different level."

Bob's savory king cake uses a hamburger bun dough and is filled with fresh Louisiana boudin, topped with bacon (though the original recipe called for fried pork skin cracklins), and finished with a drizzling of local favorite Steen's® cane syrup. The creation went viral, and Bob was contacted almost immediately to be interviewed on local television. One reporter asked him how viewers could get a boudin king cake. Bob wasn't prepared for the question. "I think I said, 'Well, if you contact me, I could make you one,'" he remembered. "I thought it was going to be ten people."

Bob was wrong. Within hours, he had more than one hundred orders. "I was literally trying to scare people away with the price," he said. "I told someone it would cost $150 plus shipping, to which she replied, 'That's ridiculous, and I need five in Los Angeles by Tuesday.'"

Using only his home oven, Bob couldn't keep up. Defeated, he was about to announce

Co-owners of Twin's Burgers & Sweets, Denny (left) and Billy Guilbeau (right) with Dr. Bob Carriker, the inventor of the boudin king cake.

his "bakery" was closed. That's when he had the idea to ask the actual bakery down the street, Twin's Burgers & Sweets, if they'd make the cakes for him. "They were known for their sweet king cakes and their burgers, so I thought maybe they'd do a savory king cake."

The owners, twin brothers Billy and Denny Guilbeau laughed as Billy remembered when Bob first approached them. "He came in and whispered, 'Can we talk in the back? I've got

an idea I think there might be some interest in,' which turned out to be an incredible understatement."

It was the middle of Carnival, and the brothers were already busy with their own king cakes, but they told him they'd give it a try when their boudin shipment arrived on Tuesday. Bob, meanwhile, relayed that information to the hordes emailing him incessantly about getting a cake. When Tuesday arrived, it was

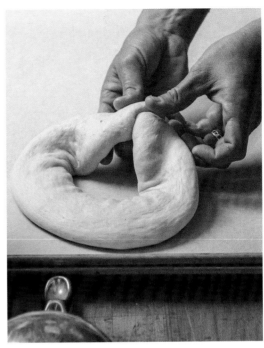

pandemonium. "We'd ordered twenty-five pounds of boudin and two dozen bottles of Steen's, and we thought we'd be fine," Billy said. "Customers were lined up out the door, and our phones were ringing off the hook with people wanting it shipped across the country. We sold out immediately." The next day they quadrupled their supplies, but the result was the same. During those last three weeks of Carnival, Twin's sold more than six thousand boudin king cakes!

"When Bob first gave us the idea, we asked if he wanted royalties," Billy remembered, "but he said just give him a gift card if the cake sold well."

Of course, it sold far better than anyone could have imagined. Does Bob regret not accepting the royalties? "Nah," he laughed, "they said I could eat for free at Twin's for life. I've been taking them up on that!"

Laurel Street Bakery

"McKenzie's had something like fifty locations so there wasn't really room for other bakeries."

Hillary Guttman's king cake journey began while studying neuroscience in Austin, Texas. A young Hillary would hit the books at her favorite coffee shops and bakeries around town. They were the kinds of businesses she hadn't seen growing up in New Orleans. "Twenty years ago, we didn't really have bakeries where you could sit with a cup of coffee and a treat," she said. "Basically, all New Orleans had was McKenzie's—great for picking up something for home, but not a place to hang out."

She enjoyed her study spots so much, Hillary took two jobs at local Austin bakeries. ("You need two jobs to afford a place in Austin anyway!" she joked...kind of.) One job was at a grocery store bakery, where she learned to decorate cakes. The other was a mom-and-pop shop where she made cakes from scratch. As Hillary's talent and passion grew, her mom encouraged her to start a bakery back in New Orleans. "But McKenzie's had something like fifty locations," she explained, "so there wasn't really room for other bakeries."

Then, on May 17, 2000, the unthinkable happened: a bad health inspection led to all McKenzie's Pastry Shoppes shutting their doors and filing for bankruptcy. An attempt the following year to revitalize the local chain failed, leaving New Orleans with a sudden dearth of bakeries. Starting a bakery of her own now seemed possible, at least in theory. Hillary moved back to New Orleans.

But buying a bakery was still financially out of reach. Instead, she took a job with gourmet catering staple Chez Nous, expanding her culinary repertoire and saving the money she'd need to eventually launch the business of her dreams.

In 2004, the opportunity finally presented itself. Hillary learned of an older woman with a bakery on Laurel Street looking to retire.

LEFT PHOTO: Bakery Owner Hillary Guttman (left) with bakers Carrie Asch (center) and Courtney Hyde. **OPPOSITE PAGE:** Laurel Street Bakery's Nutella® king cake (top) and traditional king cake.

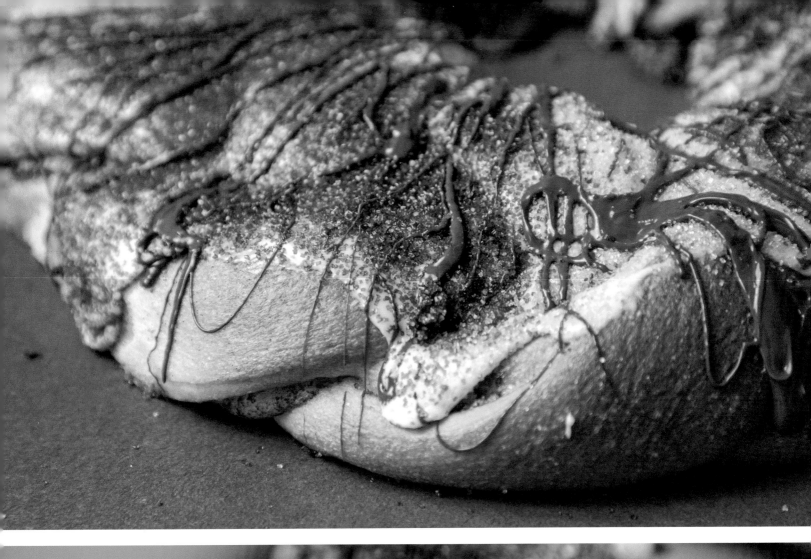

Hillary worked with her for three months, negotiated a purchase price, and took over the business, naming it Laurel Street Bakery. The operation initially was focused on selling wholesale baked goods to companies like PJ's Coffee, Royal Blend, and Perkins, but by 2013 when Hillary expanded to her current location on South Broad Avenue, Laurel Street Bakery had switched exclusively to retail.

Today, bagels are a big part of her bakery's success. But, come Carnival season, the king cakes are extremely popular, as well. Traditional king cakes are always the biggest seller, but last year Hillary tried a Nutella® king cake that flew off the shelves. She credits her cake's success to a moister dough. "A lot of bakeries still use brioche, but I opted for a homemade cinnamon roll dough full of butter, buttermilk, eggs, flour, and a little bit of sugar." In addition to texture,

cinnamon roll dough is a product Hillary already makes and has space to store. She also finds it easier than brioche to work with at a variety of temperatures. "And it's more flavorful, too!"

So grab a slice of king cake, but don't rush home. Twenty years ago, New Orleans was a place where you could only take your baked goods to go. Thanks to Hillary and her generation of twenty-first century bakers, that's no longer the case.

In just its first year, Hillary said the Nutella king cake flew off the shelves. It is both filled and topped with a generous portion of delicious Nutella spread.

Maurice French Pastries

"If I was back in France, and I could only make two types of king cake, I probably would have changed careers!"

You might presume the king cakes of a classically trained French chef would be among the more traditional in New Orleans. But Jean-Luc Albin, owner of Maurice French Pastries, has fully embraced king cake mania. He grew up the son of a talented chef in a small French Alps town. Located in the southern part of the country, this meant residents had a choice between the regionally popular gâteau des rois and the more ubiquitous galette des rois. "As young kids we liked the candied fruit and brioche of the gâteau," he said, admitting the almond frangipane in the galette may have been too sophisticated for their young palates. "Plus, the gâteau was cheaper, which made our parents happy."

Jean-Luc began working in restaurants when he was just fifteen years old. He developed his skills in Marseilles and Paris,

TOP-LEFT PHOTO: Ponchatoula strawberry king cake. **TOP-RIGHT PHOTO:** Bourbon Street king cake with a bourbon-flavored chocolate custard. **BOTTOM-RIGHT PHOTO:** Woodland Plantation king cake with Bavarian praline cream. **BOTTOM-LEFT PHOTO:** Bananas Foster-inspired General Foster king cake.

"We have our traditions, sure, but the French also approach baking and cooking like the sky's the limit."

then in the Bahamas before coming to the United States—eventually purchasing Maurice French Pastries near New Orleans in 1989 from a retiring friend.

But French or American? Which style of king cake would Jean-Luc make? Though he does produce a galette des rois, he enjoys the growing New Orleans inclination to be creative. He once designed a "Carnival Around the World" series, for example, that included a Rio

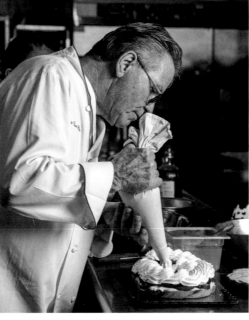

de Janeiro king cake with coffee, a Trinidad and Tobago version with rum and pineapple, and a host of others. Today, he focuses on a series of Chantilly-style king cakes, including the Ponchatoula with fresh strawberries, the Bourbon Street with a bourbon-flavored chocolate custard, the Woodland Plantation with Bavarian praline cream, and the Bananas Foster-inspired General Foster. "If I was back in France, and I could only make two types of

king cake," he laughed, "I probably would have changed careers."

Even France, Jean-Luc said, is embracing new varieties, such as a galette des rois with chocolate filling. "We have our traditions, sure, but the French also approach baking and cooking like the sky's the limit," he said. "Anything is possible in the kitchen and things and people change. That should be with king cake, too."

Nor Joe Importing Co.

"My fear is that if everyone values the eccentric, then we lose track of what made king cake special in the first place."

Mark Subervielle is the product of two renowned food cultures. One side of his family is Sicilian, part of the estimated two hundred and ninety thousand Italian immigrants arriving in New Orleans in the late nineteenth and early twentieth centuries. The other side arrived from France; his grandfather delivered milk by horse-drawn carriage along Carrollton Avenue. "Italian, French, New Orleanian," Mark listed his lineage,

Owner Mark Subervielle and sister, Rachel, with their cannoli king cake.

"it's no wonder we're passionate about food."

He purchased Nor Joe Importing Co. from its original owners in 2016, in part because it brought back memories of his past. "The cheese wheel pasta, cucidati, and muffulettas—just the smell of the shop reminded me of my grandmother's house and the stores she took us to as kids." Mark wanted Nor Joe's to be a place where those memories and traditions could be preserved.

Starting a business was an exciting endeavor, but there was a uniquely New Orleans detail Mark hadn't considered. "Carnival season was coming, and we didn't have a king cake!" he said. After a self-proclaimed mediocre attempt by Mark, his sister, Rachel, offered to give it a try. Miraculously, when she emerged from the kitchen, it was with the cannoli king cake Nor Joe's sells today. She set the sample king cake on the counter, and, within an hour, a customer bought it. "That was exciting enough," Mark said," but then the guy behind him in line wanted one, too, so we scrambled to make another."

That might have been the end of the experiment, but then a third customer came in later that day for two of Nor Joe's "famous" cannoli king cakes. The man said a coworker had just brought one to the office. Word continued to spread and soon, Mark and Rachel were hustling to keep up with lines snaking around the store.

Mark believes the king cake's popularity is due to its uniqueness, taste, and tradition. "I think people buy it the first time because there's nothing in the world like it," he said,

"then they buy it again because it's delicious." Nor Joe's king cake features a buttery brioche dough, a lot of homemade cannoli cream filling, and all the sprinkles, chocolate chips, almonds, and powdered sugar you'd expect on a cannoli. "It'd be cheaper to make if we used less cannoli cream," Mark said, "but tradition is important, and I know how much my grandma would use."

To Mark, innovating traditional foods like king cake can be exciting, but he worries too much experimentation risks forgetting beloved customs. "My fear is that if everyone values the eccentric and aims for crazy king cake versions like boudin, then we lose track of what made king cake special in the first place."

But isn't a cannoli king cake eccentric? "It's unique, sure," Mark answered, "but I don't think it's too far from what filled king cakes have been for decades. It merges our New Orleans tradition and our Italian tradition, so maybe you can't call it king cake, exactly. Maybe call it Italian king cake instead!"

172

Rickey Meche's Donut King

"I inherited a heart condition and had a replacement when I was thirty-two. I had no idea I'd live this long. Must be all the doughnuts!"

According to Lafayette, Louisiana, newspaper, *The Daily Advertiser,* eating a Meche's Donut King doughnut is the Cajun country equivalent to eating a beignet from New Orleans' Café Du Monde. It's something everyone should do. Rickey Meche's parents started the Lafayette area doughnut chain in 1969, each running a store of their own. As business thrived, they opened three more, one for each of their children. "Mom didn't want us to fight running the same business," explained Rickey, who took over his store, Rickey Meche's Donut King, in 1984. "They let us each manage our store our own way."

Rickey's way prioritized innovation. He was the first in the family to use a donut cutting machine ("My parents thought I was crazy when I bought a $40,000 machine!"), the first to create printed boxes, the first to produce kolaches, and the first to make king cakes.

"None of us had ever heard of king cake in 1984," he said. "It was a New Orleans thing."

RIGHT PHOTO: Donut cutter Nicole Domingue has worked at Rickey's shop for twenty-eight years. NEXT PAGE: The king cakes are made in much the same way as their doughnuts, including how they're filled (bottom-right photo).

Rickey first learned about them from a Pillsbury sales rep. "He said it was this oblong bread-like dough you decorate, put a baby in, and pop in the oven. But I didn't have an oven, so he suggested we fry them like our doughnuts." They glaze and fill them like doughnuts, too, with flavors such as cream cheese, Bavarian cream, blueberry, and strawberry.

Rickey's Guilbeau Road store, the last one owned by the original family, only sold about thirty king cakes in 1987, his first year selling them. But word spread and the next year Rickey couldn't make enough. Today he sells about twenty thousand in a season. And you don't even have to live in Lafayette to get one. Rickey ships so you can enjoy one (or many) of his melt-in-your-mouth doughnut king cakes wherever you reside!

175

S.S. Sweets

"For my senior project they asked us where we saw ourselves in ten years. I said I'd own a bakery in New Orleans."

It all started with an Easy-Bake Oven. "My older sister got hers first, and I was so jealous," remembered Sharena Smith, founder of home bakery, S.S. Sweets. "I finally got mine when I was seven, and oh man, that was an amazing day!" Sharena's a native of Buffalo, New York, and her love for baking extended far beyond a single toy. Every day her mother and grandmother cooked in the kitchen. Her brother, who went to trade school, came home and shared the desserts he'd made, as well as exciting details about how he made them. By the time she was eight, she was watching the Food Network, obsessively.

If Sharena had a hunch she wanted to become a baker when she was eight, she was certain of it by the time she graduated high school. And not just that she'd be baking, but where she'd be baking. After a trip to New Orleans for Essence Festival, Sharena was sure she'd be back. "For my senior project they asked us where we saw ourselves in ten years. I said I'd own a bakery in New Orleans."

Sharena returned to the city in 2014 for a three-month culinary school internship, then returned later that year for good. She was hired by a catering company run by the owners of neighborhood restaurants Tartine and Toast. During Carnival, she baked their popular cinnamon cream cheese king cake. "People from Buffalo don't know anything about king cake," she said, "so this was really my first experience, and I learned a lot." Sharena felt inspired to create a king cake of her own. She developed her preferences by watching others and by tasting popular king cakes around the city. She noticed some cakes had mass produced icing that tasted artificial and overly sweet, but she was blown away by how Dong Phuong's cream cheese icing balanced the cake's flavors.

The dough was another huge consideration. Not everyone braids their dough, but Sharena

Chef Sharena Smith prepares her crawfish king cake filled with sauteed peppers, onions, and crawfish mixed with cream cheese and shredded cheddar cheese. The king cake is topped with crawfish Monica sauce, grated parmesan cheese, and sliced green onions.

insisted. ("It's such a fun tradition!" she said.) And she learned to make king cake dough that was fluffy and full of flavor. "It doesn't matter what fillings or toppings you put on it," she said, "if the dough isn't great, your king cake can't be great."

Finally, confident in her dough, Sharena wanted to create unique flavors. She worked on multiple varieties, including Bananas Foster, pralines n' cream, sweet potato, and crawfish—flavors popular in Southern as well as African American cooking. "I wanted something more than just the sanding sugar on top," she said, finding the traditional sugar so sweet she could barely eat a slice. "I wanted toppings and fillings that felt substantial."

Sharena unveiled her king cakes in 2020, selling about one hundred, a successful year for someone baking alone from their home. The next year, thanks to word of mouth and a popular

chocolate king cake collaboration with Piety and Desire Chocolate, her sales tripled in the middle of a pandemic. The future looks bright for S.S. Sweets. But don't act surprised. Sharena predicted this years ago.

Chef Sharena Smith with her Bananas Foster king cake. The filling includes dark rum and a pureed mix of flambeed bananas in brown sugar. The cake is topped with flambeed banana cream cheese icing, caramel drizzle, and toasted candied pecans.

Chapter 5
REBIRTH

Anyone who has spent a Mardi Gras in New Orleans can attest to the sense of hope in the air. The cold, wet winter has passed, and months of parades, festivals, and beautiful weather await. But that hope isn't just a feeling. Symbols of rebirth, renewal, and a more prosperous future abound during Carnival and can be traced back millennia. After all, humans seek hope when times are challenging. And few times were more challenging for an agrarian society like early Rome than the period surrounding the winter solstice, when cold weather set in, and nights were at their longest.

But the Romans found reason for optimism. The sun would rise higher in the sky each day after the solstice, something they interpreted as the sun's rebirth. Springtime, they knew, would eventually follow. They celebrated this optimism for the future at their Saturnalia festival by planting seeds for the upcoming spring harvest and with a cake believed to be the predecessor to our king cake. Its shape—circular like the reborn sun—as well as the hidden bean and the flour it's made with all symbolize fertility and the hope of renewal.

Christians similarly anticipated springtime renewal. February 2, right in the middle of Carnival, was traditionally a day our ancestors reported to church to collect candles meant to last the remainder of winter. If the candles were long, winter was predicted to be long and difficult. If they were short, it was believed spring was near. (It's not coincidental that Groundhog's Day, which features a similar concept, is also celebrated on February 2.) While the need for candles is no longer necessary, the day is still celebrated, a welcome reminder of spring's approach. In Mexico, for example, festive tamale parties are thrown, hosted by the person who found the fève a month earlier in the Twelfth Night king cake.

Of course, renewal isn't only found after long winters. Often, it's more personal. In this chapter we see how some of our bakers overcame overwhelming challenges—whether it be homelessness, war, or uprooting to a new country—to find a rebirth of their own, with king cake often front and center.

Nolita

"My parking space was across the street from where I used to live in a tent. Eight months later I was learning to become a professional baker. It's amazing how fast life can change."

Martha Gilreath couldn't believe she was even competing in the 2020 New Orleans Wine & Food Experience. But winning the gold medal in the dessert category seemed downright unbelievable given her improbable journey. Just eighteen months earlier, Martha was homeless, sleeping under the Crescent City Connection bridge.

"I'd been homeless for eight months, but I was an addict for longer than that," she said. Cut off from her family, lonely, and miserable, Martha felt motivated to get help only once she realized, even as things got worse, she wasn't likely to die anytime soon. "I thought, geez, I don't want to do this for another thirty years." She checked into a treatment center in Charleston, South Carolina.

Residents at the center rotated through chores, and one day Martha was on dinner duty cooking for more than sixty people. Her knack for creating delicious meals out of whatever ingredients were available impressed the other

Nolita founder Martha Gilreath with her king cake under the Crescent City Connection bridge where she slept for eight months while homeless. Today she is an award-winning pastry chef.

residents. It was something she learned watching her mother cook for her and her five siblings, and it earned Martha a permanent place on the crew.

Those skills became career aspirations the day Martha was told it was a resident's twenty-first birthday. "We couldn't celebrate a big birthday the way non-addicts might," she smiled, "but we wanted to make sure he at least had a cake." Learning the resident loved cheesecake, Martha made him one, stepping outside for a cigarette once she'd finished. Martha said she'll never forget looking through

TOP PHOTO: Martha with her instructor and mentor at the New Orleans Culinary & Hospitality Institute, Pastry Chef Zak Miller. **RIGHT PHOTO:** A coarser sugar provides texture and a beautiful, vibrant color. Martha dyes the sugar herself to enhance that color.

the window and seeing his face open into a huge smile when his friends gave him the cake. "Damn, I thought, 'I want to keep making people this happy.'"

Martha returned to New Orleans in August 2020. One month later, she enrolled in the pastry program at the New Orleans Culinary & Hospitality Institute (NOCHI). "My parking space was under the Crescent City Connection, across the street from where I used to live in a tent," she said. "Now here I was, eight months later, learning to become a professional baker. It's amazing how fast life can change." At NOCHI, Martha learned the trade and developed friendships and mentors that helped her continue to grow professionally after she graduated. Upon finishing the program, Martha worked in restaurants, saving money to invest in Nolita, a bakery she co-founded five days before Carnival season.

OPPOSITE PAGE: Satsuma zest in her dough gives Martha's king cakes a brighter, citrus flavor. **TOP-LEFT PHOTO:** Proofing king cake dough doesn't only help it rise. It also enhances the cake's flavor and texture. **BOTTOM-LEFT PHOTO:** Martha adds a brown butter glaze for richness.

Her king cake has some similarities to the McKenzie's king cakes she remembered as a kid. "It tasted like a pillow of heaven," she said, laughing. Like McKenzie's, she doesn't want her king cakes to taste like a cinnamon roll, so instead of icing she uses a light layer of brown butter glaze. But that's where the similarities end. Martha uses orange blossom water and satsuma zest in her dough to give it a brighter, citrus flavor. She tops her cakes with a coarser sugar to provide texture and dyes it herself for a beautiful, vibrant color.

Since getting sober, Martha's repaired her relationship with her family and embarked on a rewarding career path. Her story is one of a life transformed, but she thinks most bakers have a story worth learning. "I've never met a baker who had the same reason for getting into the business," she said. "We're all unique, as are our journeys."

10 Cent Baking

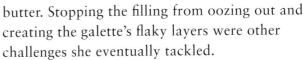

"I wanted to honor the tradition, and also put my own spin on it."

Gillian White began bartending in college. After moving to New Orleans, she continued her craft at well-respected local spots, Sylvain and Meauxbar. "What I always loved about bartending," she explained, "is how something I made with my own hands brought people so much joy."

In March 2020, the coronavirus pandemic shut down most New Orleans businesses. Without a job, but with more free time, she dove into an old hobby. Gillian had been baking sporadically for years, but now she read baking books, studied new techniques, and even explored adding flowers into her cake designs. "I draw inspiration from my experience bartending," she said, "and the flowers reminded me of garnishing a cocktail." Posting on Instagram as 10 Cent Baking, Gillian received orders for customized cakes—first from friends but quickly from strangers, too.

With Carnival season approaching, king cake became her new challenge. "I went with the galette des rois," Gillian said. "It's really an art. But a lot can go wrong, too." As a home baker, for example, she learned if her dryer was on, her kitchen got too hot for the butter. Stopping the filling from oozing out and creating the galette's flaky layers were other challenges she eventually tackled.

In addition to a traditional almond frangipane filling, Gillian offers variations filled with chocolate hazelnut or pistachio cardamom. "I wanted to honor the tradition, and also put my own spin on it," she said. Her customers appreciated her efforts, including one especially well-known James Beard award-winning chef. "Nina freakin' Compton tried one of my cakes, and then she ordered three more!"

"Because I'm self-taught, at times I suffer from imposter syndrome and self-doubt. But having so many people buy and enjoy what I bake gives me confidence I made the right decision becoming a baker."

Gillian White's galette des rois has a pistachio and cardamom filling. It's topped with flowers from local nursery, Jo Jo's Garden.

La Vie En Rose Café

"As a young, Black businesswoman raising two children on my own, that optimism resonated with me."

Kirby Jones said she'll never forget the first time she listened to the popular song, "La Vie En Rose." It was originally written by French singer Édith Piaf in 1945, but it was local trumpet legend Louis Armstrong's rendition Kirby first heard. "It's a beautiful song about seeing life, no matter how challenging, through rose-colored glasses," she said. "As a young,

Black businesswoman raising two children on my own, that optimism resonated with me."

Building her coffee-focused La Vie En Rose Café wasn't easy. Kirby hustled between daily afternoon and evening pop-ups, as well as farmers markets and catering jobs. During challenging times, she looked to another Rose. Rose Nicaud was an enslaved nineteenth century Black woman who purchased her freedom by selling coffee to French Market vendors, workers, and shoppers from a cart she pushed around the Quarter. Nicaud is an inspiration to generations of women entrepreneurs, and Kirby counts herself in that number.

"La Vie En Rose was so exhausting at first," she said, "but I believed if I worked hard, better things would come my way." And they did. In 2019, Kirby was able to set up a permanent spot inside the Contemporary Arts Center before eventually moving into a larger space, an art studio, on Oretha Castle Haley Boulevard.

Kirby's family has lived in the New Orleans area for more than three hundred years, and La Vie En Rose Café features flavors common to her Creole heritage. Her father grew up surrounded by the sugar cane fields of nearby Lutcher, Louisiana. The cafe's popular Creole latte, and the rose cane syrup used in so many of her drinks, is modeled after the flavors of those fields. Even Kirby's love for coffee comes

OPPOSITE PAGE: La Vie En Rose Café owner Kirby Jones with her two king cakes. The "Don Creole" crawfish king cake (left) is topped with shredded parmesan cheese and thyme sprigs. Kirby's "Rose Queen" cake is filled with rose syrup and cinnamon sugar, and topped with confectioners' sugar icing and edible rose petals.

from her childhood. "It was common for older generations to give their kids a sugary coffee," she said. "Though, my son's already pretty hyper, so we joke he only gets decaf."

Those inclinations toward childhood flavors extend to Kirby's baked goods, as well. In the

past, she baked her own food for the cafe, but after having her second child, she instead sells goods from local businesses like Levee Baking Company. The one thing Kirby still insists on baking are king cakes, also inspired by her past. The "Don Creole" crawfish king cake is an ode to her aunt's memorable crawfish bread, while the "Rose Queen" cake, complete with edible rose petals, uses the same nostalgic syrup found in her coffee drinks. "Keeping that history in mind as I push forward is really important to me," Kirby said.

La Vie En Rose Café was recently forced to move again, and Kirby's on the hunt for a new home for her business. It was a disappointing turn of events, but Kirby has a plan. "Until we have a new location, we'll do pop-ups around the city with our cart just like Rose Nicaud used to do," she said. "Follow us on social media to see where I'll be!" Hard work and rose-colored glasses. It's gotten Kirby this far, and it'll take her where she needs to go next, too.

Sucré

"We want our customers to taste our cream cheese filling, too. It's the balance of applying enough glaze to make the cake shine, but not so much it tastes overpowering."

When popular Magazine Street pastry shop Sucré abruptly closed in 2019, Ayesha Motwani felt that a part of New Orleans special to her and her family had gone missing. "We had so many nice memories there," she said, referring to frequent trips made to the shop with her husband, four children, and beloved goldendoodle Raja. "We missed having a place where our kids' jaws dropped to the floor when

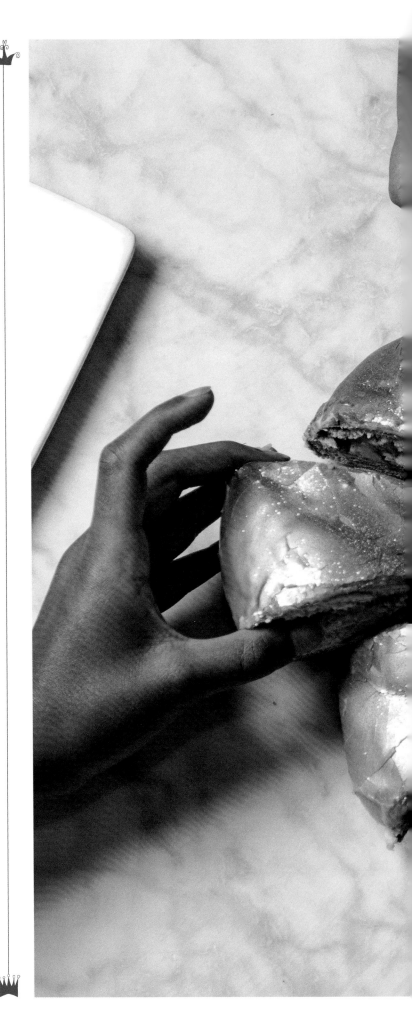

> *"When they don't think we're looking, our children lift up the cake to see if they can spot the baby, so they know what slice to ask for. Those are the exact same things we did when we were kids."*

they walked in," she said. "So, I thought, 'What if I reopened it myself?'"

That's exactly what Ayesha did in December 2020 with the help of Executive Pastry Chef Ashley McMillan. Ashley had worked at Sucré during multiple stints over the past fifteen years between positions at Commander's Palace, Bittersweet Confections, and The Ritz-Carlton. She was excited to assist in reviving the shop that helped begin her pastry career.

Sucré is known for its chic decor and a variety of colorful macarons, cakes, and gelato.

It also has one of the most recognizable king cakes in New Orleans. "We use a shiny liquid luster on our cakes to give them a metallic glaze," Ashley said. It's a remarkable, unique look, but Ashley insisted the way the glaze is applied goes beyond aesthetic. She remembers growing up in the 1990s with ultra-sweet king cakes filled "with anything you could put in a pie" and lathered in icing. Ashley gladly ate it as a child, but those memories remind her that less can be more when applying her own icing. "We want our customers to taste our cream cheese filling, too," she said. "It's the balance of applying enough glaze to make the cake shine, but not so much it tastes overpowering."

Ayesha loves playing a part in a tradition she not only experienced as a child, but that remains important to her children today. She remembers every Friday during Carnival being king cake day at school. When it was her turn to bring the cake, she and her parents stopped at the McKenzie's on Prytania Street to pick up a seven-dollar king cake. The tradition is the same today, except of course, Ayesha's children bring their king cake from Sucré. "It's so fun to watch," Ayesha said. "Last time the other students saw our cake and yelled, 'It's a different one! It's a different one!'"

At home, Ayesha's heart swells watching her children discreetly examine the cake. "When they don't think we're looking, they lift up the cake to see if they can spot the baby, so they know what slice to ask for," she laughed. "Those are the exact same things we did when we were kids."

Some traditions never change. Some get updated with a metallic glaze.

TOP PHOTO: Chef Ashley McMillan (pictured on previous spread) applies the liquid luster that gives her king cakes their signature metallic glaze. **OPPOSITE PAGE, TOP PHOTO:** Shop owner Ayesha Motwani's four children and one Goldendoodle, Raja, eye the Sucré king cake with anticipation.

Celtica French Bakery

"Sometimes you need to take a step back to jump farther."

The customs around eating king cake are generally the same in France as they are in America. There is, however, some variation in the specifics, according to Dominique Rizzo, owner of Celtica French Bakery in Lakeview. For example, in France, if the traditional galette des rois is served at a party with children, the youngest of them hides under a table and announces who gets the next piece. "So, the person distributing the cake will hold a slice up," Dominique explained, "and the child will say, 'Dominique gets the next piece!'

or whoever's turn they announce." This ensures no one can cheat and spy inside which piece the favor, or fève, is hidden. "It's such a lovely, memorable family tradition." The person who finds the fève is crowned king or queen of the party, and they're invited to choose a queen or king to serve with them.

"The galette des rois is common in France and you'll find it in every bakery during the season," Dominique said, "but I think it feels very special because the season is short." Traditionally the French would eat the galette only on January 6. Today, that's evolved. Some families eat it from the first Sunday of the year through Twelfth Night, while others enjoy it throughout January. "I think, in Louisiana, when bakeries sell king cakes all year, it loses some of what makes them unique: those special, yearned for traditions with family and friends."

As owner of Celtica, he tries to keep those special moments front of mind, because it wasn't that long ago he lost track of what was most important. Dominique was the founder and longtime owner of popular Uptown bakery, La Boulangerie. At one point he expanded to three locations, and for years it was his famous galette des rois that reintroduced a new generation of New Orleanians to the classic French king cake. "We did very good business and we got bigger and bigger and bigger," he said, "but I never slowed down, and I didn't love who I'd become by the end of that experience."

LEFT PHOTO: Chef Dominique Rizzo with his galette des rois. It's common for the galette to come with a paper crown, awarded to the guest who finds the fève.
OPPOSITE PAGE BOTTOM PHOTO: Dominique orders craft porcelain fèves from France to hide inside his cake.

"The galette des rois is common in France and you'll find it in every bakery during the season, but I think it feels very special because the season is short."

He sold the bakery in 2015 and took the time to recalibrate his values. "Sometimes you need to take a step back to jump farther," he said. Dominique took an extended break to spend time with his family and children, and to spend time in France. "It was time I desperately needed to remember what I love about baking and life, in general."

Five years later, he was ready to open another bakery, but with a renewed sense of purpose. "When I first opened La Boulangerie, there weren't many excellent bakeries in New

Orleans," he remembered. Today, Dominique said there are many, but still not enough. "Every neighborhood should have a bakery, and I want to be a neighborhood baker here in Lakeview. I want parents to come to Celtica for my fresh bread and kids to come for my pastries."

And during Carnival season, he wants families to look forward to gathering around his galette des rois. Because, just like when he was a child, that's what it's there for. "To me, king cakes are about family."

TOP ROW, SECOND PHOTO FROM LEFT: Chef Dominique adds French brand Negrita rum instead of almond extract to accentuate the almond flavor. He feels almond extract has an artificial taste. **BOTTOM ROW, MIDDLE PHOTO:** When cutting the design into the top of the unbaked cake, it's important not to cut through the dough. This would allow the almond cream to escape out of the top of the galette while baking.

Balestra's Food Center

"I want to contribute to Carnival traditions, too. King cake is my way of doing that."

"**I** poke overlapping holes in the bottom of the cake and pump the filling in through them," explained Martha Barrientos in perfect English but with an accent she brought with her when she moved from El Salvador to Louisiana. It's been a long road for Martha, and today she's the deli and bakery manager at Balestra's Food Center in the suburb of Belle Chasse. "I learned this technique from an older baker when I started with king cakes.

It allows for a lot of filling, without making the cake too messy to eat."

In a single Carnival season, Martha creates as many as twelve different varieties of king cake. This is a little ironic because Martha isn't a big fan of king cakes. "I love our dough," she quickly clarified. "It's so moist!" Sometimes, she'll enjoy a plain piece dipped in coffee before starting her shift. But why the large variety if Martha prefers plain king cake? It's because she takes great pride knowing what her customers want. "I talk to them a lot," she said. "And if they suggest making a new, interesting kind of king cake, and I think people might buy it, I'll give it a shot!"

Martha moved to south Louisiana with her five-year-old daughter in 2006 to join her then-husband who had immigrated years earlier. Martha worked at a laundromat, then in restaurants, before taking a job in the deli of a grocery store. As she rose through the store's ranks, she learned she loved decorating cakes and being creative, particularly with king cake flavors. Last year she moved to Balestra's and, when Carnival season rolled in, this meant overseeing a whole lot of king cake production.

"They were already making king cakes here before me," she said, "but I had my own way of making dough." Did the customers like it? "Well," she laughed, "they didn't stop coming to our bakery!"

King cakes aren't popular in El Salvador, and Martha said it's been exciting to learn how

LEFT PHOTO: Martha Barrientos with one of her king cakes.
OPPOSITE PAGE: Front-left, lemon blueberry king cake; back-left, traditional king cake; back-right, triple berry king cake; front-right, Oreo king cake.

"I talk to my customers a lot. And if they suggest making a new, interesting kind of king cake, and I think people might buy it, I'll give it a shot!"

to make them. She appreciates how seriously Louisiana takes celebrating Carnival and is happy to be a part of the season. "I remember my young daughter's first parade," Martha said. "People were throwing beads her way, and her eyes got as big as plates." Seeing her daughter that excited, Martha decided, "I want to contribute to Carnival traditions, too. King cake is my way of doing that."

Family living in other parts of America sometimes ask Martha if she'd want to move. She's thought about it, but when she's inventing new king cakes, attending parades, or just enjoying a Carnival season barbecue with friends and family, she knows there's only one answer. "I tell them no thank you. Louisiana is my home now."

Mayhew Bakery

"I wanted to be a soldier for the next twenty years, but life doesn't always follow plans."

When Kelly Mayhew, an eighteen-year-old boy from Charleston, South Carolina, joined the military in 2001, he had a plan that had nothing to do with baking. "I wanted to be a soldier for the next twenty years," he said, "but life doesn't always follow plans." He was on his way to basic training when hijacked airplanes hit the World Trade Center and Pentagon. Thrust into a war, Kelly served three tours in the Middle East. He damaged tendons and nerves, was hit with shrapnel in his chest, and took a bullet in a leg that, fifteen surgeries later, will never fully heal.

Kelly was medically retired in 2007 and forced to look into new career options. "Enter baking," he laughed. But it wasn't a profession totally out of left field. Kelly had grown up around baking—his grandparents founded the first Krispy Kreme® franchise (and the next nine after that). Even in the military, there were little moments that planted the seeds for a culinary career. "When I was stationed in Alaska, flights home for the holidays were too expensive," Kelly remembered, "so the other soldiers would come to my house, and I'd cook this big Christmas dinner. I loved it."

He graduated from culinary school, cooked in Charleston at some of America's best restaurants, and moved to New Orleans with his wife where he became a sous chef at Brennan's. But Kelly was formulating a new plan, and this time baking was at the heart of it. He left Brennan's to sell homemade bread at local farmers markets. Then he met his now business partner Jess Ragan-Williams, and they began baking out of a commissary in Old Metairie, doing business out of a small, makeshift service window. As Carnival approached in 2019, they engaged in a debate. "Jess is from here and wanted to make king cakes, but I was skeptical," he said. "I think they can be kind of nasty sometimes—bakeries pouring cheap icing out of buckets onto cinnamon roll dough made from mixes." But Jess insisted, and it turned

OPPOSITE PAGE: Top photo, all king cakes at Mayhew Bakery are covered in a delicious, white chocolate and honey poured fondant; bottom photo, the strawberry-Nutella® king cake is a popular variety. **RIGHT PHOTO:** Co-owners Kelly Mayhew (right) and Jess Ragan-Williams.

out she was right. They sold enough king cakes that season to move into the Mid-City shop that houses Mayhew Bakery today.

And these king cakes are far from nasty. Jess and Kelly use a white chocolate and honey poured fondant over their secret brioche dough recipe. Strawberry-Nutella® is a popular filling at Mayhew, but flavors are determined by the ingredients available from the farmers market that day. "Sometimes we have to adjust our plan," Kelly said. Over the years, it's a lesson he's learned first-hand.

TOP PHOTOS: In their strawberry-Nutella king cake, Mayhew Bakery pipes in strawberry filling on one side and Nutella filling on the other before incorporating the two by braiding the dough.

What is Twelfth Night?

In other parts of the world, it's called King's Day, Three King's Day, or Epiphany. In New Orleans, however, it's most often referred to as Twelfth Night. Here, the day is celebrated as a beginning, the first day it's socially acceptable to eat king cake and the start of Carnival's long march toward Fat Tuesday. But Twelfth Night as a prelude is new. For nearly fifteen centuries Catholics have seen the holiday as an end, the final feast of the Twelve Days of Christmas between December 25 and Epiphany.

Those twelve days commemorate the time between Jesus' birth and when the titular Three Kings—also known as the Three Wise Men or the Three Magi—found the Christ child and presented to him their gifts of gold, frankincense, and myrrh. This was the moment God revealed himself to the world through the incarnation of his son, a pivotal event in Christianity's history. Except no one actually knew what time of year Jesus was born or when to celebrate.

As Christianity gained popularity, its leaders decided it would be smarter to absorb pagan traditions than eliminate them, so the church aligned its holidays to those of ancient festivals. They wanted a special one to celebrate the origin of Christ and there was no bigger pagan festival than Saturnalia, honoring the god of the harvest and celebrating the return of the sun after the year's longest nights. Christmas and Epiphany borrow traditions from Saturnalia, including feasting, indoor trees, mischief and merrymaking, costuming, and present giving. Even the cake Romans hid their lucky bean inside became king cake, titled after the same Three Kings that gave King's Day its name.

It's only in recent centuries that Christmas was elevated in stature over Twelfth Night. In fact, for children in places like Spain and Mexico, January 6 still remains the bigger celebration, a day when the Three Kings deliver presents. It's beloved in New Orleans, as well, but for a different reason. As king cakes are eaten and parades are watched, New Orleanians aren't celebrating the end of Christmas, but the start of their favorite season of the year.

213

Café Reconcile

"In New Orleans, people buy their king cake like they buy their mayo. The kind you had as a kid is the kind you like best."

Noel Barras is the director of catering and events at Café Reconcile. During Carnival, her department handles king cake production, a task in which Noel's found an unexpected challenge. "In New Orleans, people buy their king cake like they buy their mayo," she said. "The kind you had as a kid is the kind you like best. Nothing else stacks up because you can't compete with memory."

It was a savvy decision, then, for Café Reconcile to go outside the box with their incomparable muffuletta king cake, modeled after the popular local sandwich created by Sicilian immigrants.

But, at this Central City cafe who makes the food is just as important as what they make. In addition to a restaurant and catering company, Café Reconcile is a training program

Café Reconcile staff Noel Barras (left) and Anna Rainey (right) with interns from the hospitality industry training program. The cafe makes a muffuletta king cake stuffed with local Chisesi ham, Genoa salami, mortadella, provolone cheese, and the traditional muffuletta olive salad. The king cake is based on the muffuletta sandwich which was invented in 1906 in New Orleans as the city attracted hundreds of thousands of Italian immigrants, mostly from Sicily.

214

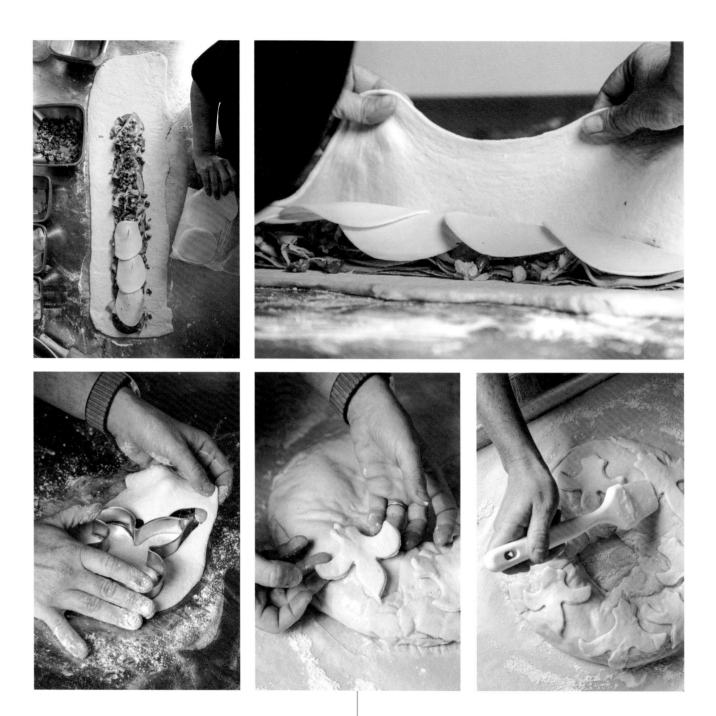

helping at-risk youth build the skills needed to gain employment in the hospitality industry. In twenty-five years, the program boasts two thousand graduates. Students work in the cafe, participate in life skills classes, and gain experience in Noel's catering department. And the muffuletta king cake, she said, is the perfect food for catering. "It's got some local flare, it's awesome for parties, and it's practical because it stays delicious all day on the parade route."

New Orleans is full of traditionalists and Noel counts herself in that number. But she thinks king cake shows the city has a willingness to experiment. "Of course you'll have people who only want the king cakes of their childhood," she said, "and that's great. But I think a lot of this city has enjoyed seeing bakers start with the tradition and express themselves from there. It's been fun for us and our students to take part."

Little J's Donuts N' More

"People talk so much about how they love those damn colors in my cake. They can't get enough of it."

"This is for my son," said Joshua Dean, who opened Little J's Donuts N' More last year in Harahan. "Most people who knew me thought I'd be in jail by the time I was forty, but when I had a kid, I wanted something positive I could pass down to him. This is it."

In between a life of partying (sometimes forcing him to live out of his car), Joshua was able to build a career in donuts that's spanned twenty-six years. Except for the past year, he's spent that time working for someone else. That

didn't stop his entrepreneurial spirit, though. Even working for others, Joshua pushed himself to create new donut flavors and a king cake that met his high expectations.

"When I was a kid, I loved the festivities and traditions around Mardi Gras and king cake, but I hated the taste," Joshua said. "They tasted like dry cinnamon rolls." As a baker, he's strived to create something he truly liked by using donut dough instead of the common sweet dough, by kneading it longer, and by frying it like a donut. His recipe resulted in a moister, denser king cake that's won awards at the annual King Cake Festival.

Joshua's final touch is coloring the dough purple, green, and gold so customers can see the colors of Mardi Gras—not just in the colored sugar on top—but also when they cut into the cake. "People talk so much about how they love those damn colors in my cake," he laughed, "they can't get enough of it."

Joshua still enjoys inventing new king cakes. He makes a version that weaves in bacon as he braids the dough. Another is a nod to the old McKenzie's cake, just the tri-colored sugar without icing that was so popular in New Orleans throughout most of the twentieth century.

With help from the local Jefferson Parish Economic Development Commission, Joshua opened his shop in Harahan, just outside of

OPPOSITE PAGE: One unique aspect of Little J's king cakes is that owner Joshua Dean dyes the dough purple, green, and gold; top-left, for one of his specialty king cakes, Joshua braids bacon with the multi-colored dough.

New Orleans. It's near where he spent days playing as a kid and now his four-year-old son Jacen plays there, too. "It's his face on our logo, and he loves it," Joshua laughed. "He'll come in and say, 'Daddy! It's me!' And he's right, it is. This whole thing's for him."

Little J's is truly a family affair. Joshua's dad, Jack, works with Joshua at the shop. And Jacen can often be found there. "Who knows?" Josh said, smiling. "Maybe one day Jacen will pass Little J's to his child—and maybe that kid will have some name that starts with J, too."

TOP PHOTO: A framed photo of Joshua Dean and his son Jacen hangs on the wall as customers enjoy Little J's king cake.

221

Viva Las Vegan

"*I loved my life away from NOLA, but I also missed the culture, the music, the Mardi Gras Indians. I came home.*"

For someone to use the phrase "Ichiwawa" out loud, I figured that person must have lived a sheltered, happy-go-lucky life, free of adversity. Then I met Gregory Felio along the Mississippi River at Crescent Park. "Ichiwawa, it's hot out here!" he said, carrying three of his vegan king cakes toward me.

But Gregory's life hasn't been without adversity. In fact, quite the opposite. The success of his business, Viva Las Vegan, is a direct result of Gregory's resilience. In spite of everything he's been through, he's overflowing with energy and optimism. That's the kind of guy, I learned, who uses "Ichiwawa" in a sentence.

Gregory grew up in New Orleans. Burning with a desire to see the world, he took a job cooking on a cruise ship when he was eighteen years old. "Everyone working on that ship seemed like they wanted something out of life," Gregory said. "Man, that was exactly the kind of energy I needed right then."

Years later, he returned to the South, now with a family. "I loved my life away

TOP PHOTO: Gregory Felio with his two sons and three king cakes along the Mississippi River in Crescent Park; **OPPOSITE PAGE:** Mardi Gras Indian, Aaron "Flagboy Giz" Hartley with Viva Las Vegan's Zulu king cake.

"I believe God has given me the gift to touch people with plant-based food."

from NOLA, but I also missed the culture, the music, the Mardi Gras Indians. I came home." Gregory cooked at pop-ups and then bought a food truck. He focused on vegan cooking after watching the documentary, *What The Health* and felt like he finally found his calling. "I believe God has given me the gift to touch people with plant-based food."

But realizing his gift hasn't been easy. At the same time Gregory's created vegan burgers, wings, pizzas, and king cake, he's had to persevere through broken down food trucks, robberies, and the struggle to find a reliable location from which to sell food.

It's the optimism and persistence that get him through. "I was put here to help people with my food," he said, "and I've seen my cooking turn a person's day around."

Gregory said when he was a child, king cake had that effect on him, and he'll do almost anything to ensure his plant-based king cakes do the same for others. "When a customer requested a vegan cream cheese king cake, I made a vegan cream cheese king cake. When they asked for fruit filling, I made one with fruit filling. And when they ask me to ship across the country, I do that, too. I'm here to serve. Nothing can stop me."

OPPOSITE PAGE: Viva Las Vegan's cinnamon cream cheese king cake is vegan, organic, and can be made gluten-free.

Chapter 6

INGREDIENTS AND SKILL

As our tastes, technology, and ideas have evolved over the centuries, so too has our king cake. It's impossible to say exactly what Louisiana king cakes looked like in the eighteenth and early-nineteenth centuries, but having been brought here by Spanish and southern French immigrants, something akin to the ring-shaped, fruit-studded, brioche roscón de reyes and gâteau de rois are good guesses.

King cakes popularized by the turn of the twentieth century, in part because of its growing association with Carnival season instead of only Twelfth Night. Bakeries, looking to help their king cakes stand out, advertised in local newspapers and decorated their cakes with colorful candies and sugar. Some described cakes with fondant candies piled high in the center while a January 6, 1948, *New Orleans Item* article detailed a "round coffee cake with a hole in the top like a doughnut...decorated with sugar and red, green, and white anise seeds and citron." About this time, McKenzie's became among the first, if not the first, to regularly use Carnival colored sugar. Their king cake became the standard, a lightly sweetened brioche with no cinnamon or icing. Generations of New Orleanians ate this king cake in the morning with their coffee, sometimes scraping butter onto their slice.

American tastes shifted toward more sugary foods in the decades after World War II. King cake bakers adjusted. Beginning in the 1960s, many experimented with sweeter doughs like cinnamon roll dough. The following decade, icing became a common king cake fixture, and recipes for praline varieties could be found in *The Times-Picayune*. By the 1980s, sweet fillings common in doughnuts and pastries such as strawberry, blueberry, and Bavarian cream were added, and the king cake's evolution to its present form was nearly complete.

Today, the variety of king cakes seems endless. While some bakeries focus on the wild and crazy, others appeal to history and tradition. Either way, king cake is in great hands with the bakers in this chapter. They wowed us with their unique vision for the constantly evolving cake, and their commitment to the ingredients and skill needed to bring that vision to life.

Blue Bowls NOLA

"Something I made myself could make people happy, and I could earn a living? I wanted to keep doing that!"

Lizza Dufrene loves trying new things. King cake, however, wasn't one of them. She grew up in Houston, where she found the popular grocery store versions to be dry and bland. But when she met Andre, a proud Louisianian and her now-husband, he brought her one she loved so much she nearly ate it all herself.

When I first found Lizza's food truck, Blue Bowls NOLA, I didn't even know they sold king cake. It was the suggestive name and amazing tater tots that caught my attention. The quality of the food was especially surprising given how recently Lizza had begun her cooking career.

Before the coronavirus pandemic, Lizza was employed selling art at a Frenchmen Street market. Soon art wasn't all she was selling. "The vendors at the art market looked like they needed some delicious, inexpensive food,"

Lizza Dufrene and her daughter, Nana, add the icing to their Blue Bowls NOLA king cake.

Lizza recalled. "So, one day I showed up with two crock pots of homemade soup, one with meat and the other vegan." She sold the soup for five dollars a serving in blue, plastic bowls. "When I handed one of my friends a bowl of soup, he said, 'Thanks for giving me blue bowls, Lizza!' And our name was born!"

Lizza quickly realized she could make more money selling soup than art. "It felt amazing to have other people enjoy my food," she said. "Something I made myself could make people happy, and I could earn a living? I wanted to keep doing that!" When the pandemic shut down the art market, Lizza continued to prepare food and deliver meals. Andre used a pandemic small business loan to purchase the food truck they use today.

Never satisfied, Lizza continued to expand her repertoire. She learned to bake, developing an appreciation for vegan baking. "It's just so much more moist," she said, "I really do prefer it." During Carnival, Lizza combined her newfound loves of king cake and vegan baked goods. "It's how I embraced my new hometown," she said. "When I saw everyone going bonkers for king cake, I wanted to make that, too, but in my own special way." In her lemon cream cheese king cake, she uses almond milk instead of cow's milk, flax seed instead of eggs, and a vegan lemon curd filling.

The food truck can be found parked outside bars and music venues across the city. Lizza takes orders on social media at Blue Bowls NOLA. That's also where you can see what new and exciting things she's cooking up next. Because with Lizza, there's always something new and exciting going on.

OPPOSITE PAGE: The Blue Bowls NOLA lemon cream cheese king cake is completely vegan, made with almond milk, flax seed, and a vegan lemon curd filling.

Breads on Oak

"For nearly a decade we've worked tirelessly to show our customers plant-based food can be delicious. And not just delicious, but the most delicious."

Everything served at Breads on Oak, including their king cake, is organic and vegan. So why is it that the majority of New Orleanians who purchase these popular king cakes aren't actually vegan themselves? Maybe it's reputation: the bakery has won multiple awards at the annual Ogden Museum King Cake Walk. Or maybe it's the quality of the ingredients: Breads on Oak is meticulous about creating vegan alternatives to products like cream cheese that are at least as good as their dairy counterparts.

But co-owner Sean O'Mahony said, above all, the success of their king cakes comes down to word of mouth. "For nearly a decade we've worked tirelessly to show our customers plant-based food can be delicious," he said. "And not just delicious, but the most delicious. When our customers are trying to win their king cake party, they come to us. Not because we're vegan, but because we make their favorite cake."

A classically trained baker from The French Pastry School in Chicago, Sean remembers taking trips to New Orleans in the late 80s and early 90s. He was inspired by the city's old bakeries. "La Bonbonniere just down the street was owned by an Austrian man, Croissant d'Or was opened by the incredible Maurice Delechelle, and Gambino's made our wedding cake," Sean recalled. "There's a long line of legendary bakers in New Orleans to aspire to."

Sean insisted his primary goal isn't to make food that's vegan. It's to make food that rises to the example set by those giants of New Orleans baking. It just so happens, he said, excellence and vegan baking can be one in the same. "It's better for our customer's health, it's better for the environment, it's better for animals," he said, "and also vegan baking tastes great. It's so much moister!"

Chef Sean O'Mahony with three of his stuffed, vegan king cakes: bourbon praline pecan, cream cheese, and almond frangipane.

Baking vegan, however, isn't always easy. Sean starts by tasting non-vegan options to give himself a clear vision of what he's trying to match or surpass. He then begins the long process of creating a vegan recipe and learning to replicate it. His first king cake took weeks to perfect. Today, he has nearly a dozen options—from traditional cinnamon, to filled varieties like cream cheese and chocolate tiramisu, to boozy cakes like brandy berry almond cream and bourbon praline pecan. "I'm first generation Irish," Sean laughed. "I had to have a few boozy ones." Some of his cakes are alcoholic and some aren't, but they're all vegan.

The most beautiful element of his king cakes is the colored sugar. "Sugar is sometimes treated with bone char," Sean said, "so we had to find another way." He uses sanding sugars made from colorful plant-based ingredients. The purple is made from beets, the green from cabbages, and the gold from turmeric and annatto.

If you're not convinced a vegan king cake is for you, Sean hopes you'll give it a try. "My goal is when someone tries our king cake, it doesn't even cross their mind it's vegan. It's just a delicious, exceptional king cake."

OPPOSITE PAGE, BOTTOM PHOTO: Because sugar is often treated with bone char, Breads on Oak uses sanding sugars made from colorful plant-based ingredients. The purple is made from beets, the green from cabbages, and the gold from turmeric and annatto.

Passion Flour Baked Goods

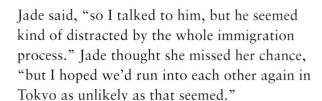

"When we started going to New Orleans farmers markets, we weren't only introduced to amazing local ingredients, but to amazing people, as well."

A "meet cute" is a scene, usually in a movie or television series, in which two characters who form a romantic connection first interact. Romeo Montague and Juliet Capulet had a meet cute. Harry Burns and Sally Albright had a meet cute. And Jade Guidotti and Ryder Hersh, co-founders of Passion Flour Baked Goods, had a meet cute, too.

Ryder attended Loyola University in New Orleans while Jade studied in Florida, but they met in the immigration line in Tokyo, each about to start their study abroad semester. "I saw him standing in line and thought he was so cute,"

Jade said, "so I talked to him, but he seemed kind of distracted by the whole immigration process." Jade thought she missed her chance, "but I hoped we'd run into each other again in Tokyo as unlikely as that seemed."

Fast forward about an hour later to Jade meeting her flatmate, who happened to be... Ryder! That was nine years ago. They became friends, started dating, got married and have done a lot of traveling. They moved to France, Finland, Vermont, and Hawaii, mostly working on farms and always collecting tips and recipes for converting the fresh produce they were surrounded by into delicious meals and baked goods.

When they arrived in New Orleans, the couple worked at several coffee shops and bakeries. But what they really wanted was to start a bakery of their own. Unfortunate circumstances would soon make that possible. "Like a lot of people in the service industry, we both got laid off when the coronavirus pandemic hit," Jade said. "That really lit a fire in us to start Passion Flour."

They sold their pastries at farmers markets, where they were introduced to new sources of local ingredients. "We had access to things like goat milk, zucchini, squash, peaches, and strawberries," Jade said, "but it also introduced us to some amazing people." Whereas Jade and Ryder felt larger bakeries could sometimes get too

Passion Flour Baked Goods co-owners Jade Guidotti and Ryder Hersh sell their pastries at farmers markets around the city, including a weekend market at Disco Warehouse. The couple takes pride in buying locally whenever possible. Much of the produce in their baked goods comes from the Indian Springs Farmers Association and The Pickle Kid. Jade's dress is from Slowdown, and her earrings and hat pin are from IDJV Art and Jewelry.

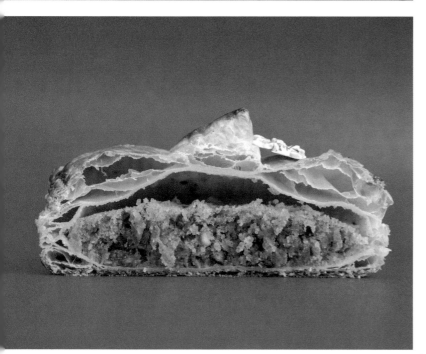

competitive with one another, the vendors they'd see at weekly neighborhood markets became collaborators who shared similar goals and values. "These are special people who are genuine, kind, and caring. They make healthy and wholesome food, they pay their workers a livable wage, and they support other small businesses."

Ryder and Jade take those values to heart. When I visited them at the farmers market, their blackberry nutmeg cream king cake and galette des rois were full of ingredients from local farms,

their fèves came from local shop Grit and Luster Ceramics, and even Jade's clothes and jewelry were from local makers. "We believe the world's better when we buy locally," Jade said, "and that starts with our own actions."

TOP PHOTOS: A galette des rois (left) and blackberry nutmeg cream king cake. All fèves are created locally by Grit and Luster Ceramics.

Why Purple, Green, and Gold?

Times-Picayune journalist Lily Jackson credits McKenzie's Pastry Shoppes as the first to consistently use purple, green, and gold sugar to decorate a king cake in the 1930s and '40s. But where did those three colors come from and how did they become so important to Carnival?

It began in 1872 with the founding of the Rex Organization. New Orleans was struggling to recover from the economic effects of the Civil War and hoped Carnival tourism would help. Unfortunately, Fat Tuesday had devolved into chaotic, dangerous street parties and the city considered shutting it down. Enter Rex, promising a safer, more organized celebration without sacrificing its signature merrymaking.

Rex means king in Latin and all kingdoms need a flag. Tricolor flags were common—think Great Britain, France, and the United States—but why purple, green, and gold? Theories abound. One incorrectly suggests it's because Rex wanted to incorporate the colors of the house sigil of the visiting Grand Duke Alexei Alexandrovich of Russia. (The sigil doesn't include purple or green, in fact.) Others connect them to the colors of the Catholic liturgy during Lent. Still others note that sigils must alternate colors (purple, for royalty) and metals (gold, symbolic of wealth and power), but why green as the final color?

While the colors' earliest roots are unclear, Rex used its 1892 Carnival parade, called "Symbolism of Colors," to assign the meaning so many New Orleanians know today: purple for justice, gold for power, and green for faith.

Rex worked hard throughout the late nineteenth century to get New Orleanians on board, issuing proclamations in local newspapers imploring them to "SHOW THE KING'S COLORS." And it worked. A 1902 *Times-Picayune* article described, "All over the city these colors are seen... They stream from veranda and housetop; they hang from the handlebars of the cyclists' wheels; they flutter in the breeze from the front of the whizzing electric cars; they are even tied to the flowing mane and prancing steed and are...worn by nearly every person in the city as well."

Today, purple, green, and gold are no longer just the colors of Rex, but the colors of the entire Carnival season, king cake included.

Coffee Science

"If something we bake has the word 'coffee' in the name, I want you to really taste the specific kind of coffee we've chosen. That's what we're going for with our king cakes."

Tom Oliver, owner of Coffee Science in Mid-City doesn't care much for coffee-flavored treats that only vaguely taste like coffee. "If something we bake has the word 'coffee' in the name," he said, "I want you to really taste the specific kind of coffee we've chosen. That's what we're going for with our king cakes."

Coffee Science opened in January 2018, but Tom's been in the business for much longer than that. Since the late 1980s, he's sold coffee beans, trained baristas, serviced equipment, managed a beloved former French Quarter shop named Kaldi's, and co-owned wholesale roaster Orleans Coffee. Having experience in so many steps of the coffee-making process allowed Tom, a physics major in college, to put his coffee-making philosophy to work. "To me, coffee is a science," he explained. "I want it to be the same every time." After decades in the industry, Tom has the knoweldge to do exactly that by choosing the precise beans he wants, and by purchasing and adapting equipment that allows him to roast those beans in a very specific way.

The only aspect of Tom's shop in which he didn't have experience was baking the treats that went along with his coffee. But the coronavirus pandemic changed that, forcing him to fill the role of baker himself. He turned to the same principles of perfection and replication that he learned on the coffee side of the business. "You try things out until you find something you like," he said, "and then you learn to replicate." In coffee, that means finding high-quality beans. With food, he said, it means seeking out fresh, local ingredients that allow him to spur the New Orleans economy while producing a better-tasting, consistent product.

That, he believes, is what makes Coffee Science's baked goods so popular. And that popularity gave him the idea, in 2018, to

OPPOSITE PAGE: Top photo, chocolate espresso king cake filled with a chocolate espresso ganache; bottom photo, mixed berry and cream cheese king cake made with local berries.

begin baking king cakes. "We're in a little bit of a baked goods desert on this side of Broad Avenue," he said, "and we have all these public defenders and schoolteachers coming in every morning. Offices and schools need king cake, so I figured let's go for it."

Tom's twist on king cake comes from incorporating his most popular coffee drinks into the fillings. Chocolate espresso and Venetian cream are two of his best-selling varieties, and he uses a concentration six times as strong as espresso to ensure the flavor isn't lost while baking.

Next, he hopes to incorporate single origin coffee into his king cakes, meaning all the coffee in an order comes from the same place. Since each variety is from a single source, the king cake will be identified by name and taste based on the origin of the beans. "I think it would be so cool," Tom said. "Your Guatemalan coffee king cake would have notes of graham cracker and chocolate because that's how those beans taste. Costa Rican king cake might have notes of strawberry and lime. I could go on forever, but you should stop by and taste it for yourself."

Compagnon Bakery

"This quality of flour doesn't exist anywhere else in the region, and it really makes a difference. It's why our products are so fresh and full of flavor."

When it came time for a bakery or restaurant to create their king cake for our book, most had a single expert king cake-maker they leaned on to produce the perfect, photogenic cake. Not so at Compagnon Bakery. "Do you want to make the dough or should I?" Quinn Berger asked Andrew Roth while we were preparing to photograph at the bakers' Lower Garden District home. In this two-person operation, they're both experts.

Andrew and Quinn met while working at popular Austin bakery, Easy Tiger. Because of the large number of New Orleanians living in Texas' capital city, that's also where they learned to make king cakes. "Honestly, I was kind of 'meh' on king cakes at first," Andrew smiled. "You don't really get it until you come to New Orleans and see firsthand how people love it, and the sheer variety available."

After Easy Tiger, they both took jobs at the nearby Barton Springs Mill. The Austin-area business' signature flour is one of the keys to Compagnon's quality. If you've eaten bread, a pastry, or a king cake made by Quinn or Andrew, you can literally taste the lessons they learned during this time. The mill works with farmers across Texas to produce flour from heirloom seeds, meticulously examined and passed down generation after generation. The result is that when you take a bite of king cake from Compagnon Bakery, you're eating

TOP PHOTO: Bakers Andrew Roth (left) and Quinn Berger with their traditional king cake. They place a priority on high-quality, organic ingredients. For example, their king cakes are topped with organic sugar turned purple, green, and gold with plant-based dyes.

a product derived from the same healthy, high-quality crops grown in Texas more than one hundred years ago. "This doesn't exist anywhere else in the region, and there's probably only a half-dozen people who do it in the whole country," Andrew explained. "It really makes a difference. It's why our products are so fresh and full of flavor."

In addition to tasting better, their flour is also healthier. Unless the grain is certified organic, Andrew said you have to assume the worst. That

can include all sorts of unnatural additives. As more Americans discover food allergies, they don't know what ingredients to blame. Unknown additives and the generally opaque practice of grain growing and milling can leave consumers clueless as to which ingredients are actually causing their allergic reaction. Andrew and Quinn solve this with Barton Springs' flour, which avoids unnatural additives, as well as pesticides, another common treatment at other mills. "Whoever makes your bread, the grain is

probably coming directly from the mill," Andrew explained. "So anything you spray on it—pesticides included—aren't going away. That's what you're eating."

Quinn and Andrew moved to New Orleans in 2019, but they fell in love with the city's food culture on visits before that. Now, they're a part of that culture. And they're taking their preference for high-quality, organic ingredients and merging it with their new home's traditions. They top their king cakes with organic sugar, for

example, dying it purple, green, and gold with plant-based dyes.

Their high standards make a difference, and you'll taste it in their cinnamon-filled traditional king cake, as well as other varieties including a strawberry hibiscus king cake and a café au lait version. Andrew and Quinn are working to find a permanent storefront, but in the meantime, you can visit the duo at farmers markets around town. In the past, they've even offered delivery directly to their customers' homes.

Creme Confectionery

"I sold five hundred king cakes last year, and I may not remember all my customers' names, but I remember their allergies."

In the world of New Orleans baking, Nicole Maurer was on a traditional path toward excellence. She attended the John Folse Culinary Institute and took jobs in esteemed pastry departments at Haydel's, Swiss Confectionery, the New Orleans Country Club, and The National WWII Museum. Six years ago, however, her path was interrupted. Nicole was diagnosed with celiac disease, an immune reaction that prevented her from eating gluten.

"Selfishly at first, I started teaching myself how to bake gluten-free so I could keep enjoying the pastries and cakes I loved," she said. But Nicole was surprised to discover two million other Americans also suffer from celiac. "I wanted to learn to bake this way for them, too."

As she learned, Nicole's eyes were opened to how many different food allergies people struggle with; individuals who can't eat gluten, dairy, nuts, soy, eggs, oat, and more. She wanted them each to have bakery options as well, so she worked tirelessly taking hundreds of recipes she loved—for eclairs, petit fours, doberge, cakes, pies, and cookies—and adjusting them in multiple ways for people with multiple allergies.

All that adjusting can get complicated. "If a customer has a dairy allergy, I use oat milk because it's closest in thickness to cow's milk," Nicole explained, "but if they have an oat allergy, I use almond milk. If they have a nut *and* an oat allergy, I use rice milk, but then I have to adjust the rest of the recipe because rice milk is so thin." These variations require Nicole to go to six grocery stores each week for the products she needs, stocking her kitchen with fifteen different specialty flours.

And on top of it all, of course, Nicole wants her baked good to taste great; not only for her customers, but also for the non-allergic friends enjoying the treats with them. She's won several awards for her extraordinary baking, including for her king cake.

LEFT PHOTO: Pastry Chef Nicole Maurer of Creme Confectionery with her traditional cinnamon king cake.

It's a lot of work for one person, but Nicole said each phone call, website query, and farmers market customer reminds her it's worth it. "I sold five hundred king cakes last year, and I may not remember all my customers' names, but I remember their allergies." Nicole said it's personal to her. "It breaks my heart, the idea of a child with a certain allergy going without a birthday cake or a king cake."

Thanks to Nicole, they won't have to.

Nicole also makes an award-winning brown butter king cake. All of Creme Confectionery's products are gluten-free and can be adapted to meet multiple dietary needs.

Adrian's Bakery

"What really sets the best king cakes apart is having the expertise to deal with your dough when the conditions aren't perfect. Because, in Louisiana, the conditions are never perfect!"

Each morning Adrian Darby listens to the radio on the short commute from his Gentilly home to his bakery. Three years ago, when he got in the car, the morning show happened to be announcing their pick for New Orleans' best king cake. "They said 'Adrian's Bakery,'" he smiled, "and I agree, but it was still nice to hear."

Adrian's been baking for more than thirty years. "That's enough time to learn some things," he said. "Everyone makes their king cakes a little differently—like some put the sugar on before baking and some afterwards—but what really sets the best king cakes apart is having the expertise to deal with your dough when the conditions aren't perfect. Because guess what? In Louisiana, the conditions are never perfect!" As a result of decades of accumulated knowledge, Adrian knows how to respond when the temperature in the bakery is too hot or too cold, or when the humidity's not ideal. He knows that a filled king cake requires less icing than a plain king cake, and that most king cakes labeled "too dry" are actually just overbaked.

That's not knowledge you attain overnight. Adrian began baking at the landmark Woolworth's department store on Canal Street in 1987. Within six months, at just twenty-two years old, he was promoted to bakery supervisor managing employees over twice his age. During the next decade, Adrian led some of the most popular New Orleans bakeries of the 1990s—inside grocery stores like Canal Villere and Robért Fresh Market, as well as independent shops such as the legendary Lawrence's Bakery.

In 2000, he opened Adrian's Bakery in the same shopping plaza it sits today, though his customer base has grown exponentially. He sells more than thirteen thousand king cakes in a year from his bakery and the eleven local stores to which he delivers.

"People know me, and they know I'm going to give them a great king cake," he said, "because I've been doing this for a very long time."

LEFT PHOTO: Adrian Darby with his praline king cake.
OPPOSITE PAGE: Constructing the supreme king cake. Cream cheese is pumped into the whole cake with strawberry, lemon, pineapple, and apple each added to a different quadrant. At Adrian's Bakery, the colored sugar is added before the icing.

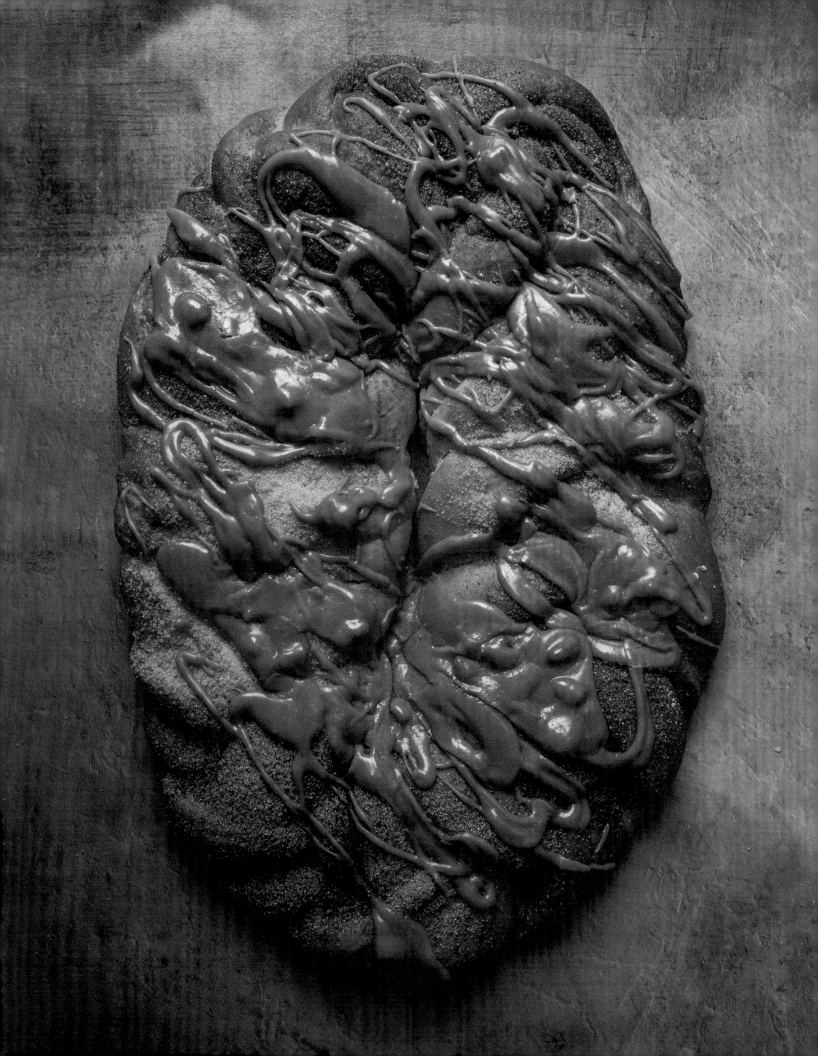

Piety and Desire Chocolate

"My philosophy is if you're not making king cake during Mardi Gras, you're missing out!"

Chocolatier Chris Nobles, owner of Piety and Desire Chocolate, is known for his chocolate works of art. But king cake has been part of his life for even longer. He was born on Bacchus Sunday and went home from the hospital on Mardi Gras. "Basically, every birthday cake I've ever had has been king cake," he said. "I probably lived off it in utero!" Chris is originally from Kenner "Kenner, *bruh*," he corrected me, emphasizing the local parlance) and he grew up on classic king cakes like Haydel's and Randazzo's.

But it was chocolate that captured the heart of a young Chris. His grandfather opened a small grocery after World War II. Chris remembers grandpa visiting on Sundays with goodie bags full of chocolates like Reese's Peanut Butter Cups. But it was a study abroad semester in Belgium that moved Chris from a casual chocolate fan to a full-blown chocolate aficionado. "Some people think Belgium is the chocolate capital of the world, and I think that's overblown," he said, "but it was a lot better than anything I could get in New Orleans at the time. I was hooked."

As a behavioral therapist in 2014, Chris frequently brought nicer bars of chocolate to eat with lunch. Seeing his passion, a coworker asked if he'd ever made his own chocolate. "I remember scoffing like, 'What?! You can't just make your own chocolate!'" But after a quick online search, Chris found an active community of people doing just that. He joined them, repurposing small kitchen gadgets for chocolate production. His interest growing, he enrolled in classes and visited farms in Central America where cacao was grown.

OPPOSITE PAGE: A slice of "Da Crown" king cake, resting on a bed of cocoa nibs and surrounded by king cake bonbons. The bonbons are made from scratch using organic lemon peel, cinnamon sticks, and premium vanilla.

By November 2017, Chris was ready to open shop, and Piety and Desire Chocolate quickly became the go-to spot for "bean to bar" chocolate and beautiful, creatively flavored bonbons. After a successful opening, Chris was ready to revisit an old friend: king cake.

"My philosophy is if you're not making king cake during Mardi Gras, you're missing out!" he said, adding, "I jumped at the chance to merge chocolate with one of my favorite traditions." He used his creative chocolate flavors to make a tiki king cake, a Star Wars-themed variety, and collaborations with other local king cake-makers like S.S. Sweets, Rahm Haus, and Que Pasta Nola. "There are so many talented New Orleanians," he said. "Why not work with them?"

Chris' main king cake is "Da Crown." "Because it's a crowning achievement in the evolution of king cake," Chris said. "No, just kidding, it's because it symbolizes the Carnival themes of decadence and royalty." The oval-shaped chocolate dough mimics a crown, studded with jewels of candied kumquats and king cake flavored bonbons. An Earl Grey ganache filling also evokes royalty, as do the cocoa nibs, reserved in Aztec society for the elite. Chris adds pink peppercorn to symbolize the decadence of the Old World spice trade.

"The symbolism is a lot of fun," Chris said, "but really it's a chance to show my devotion to three things I love very much: chocolate, king cake, and Mardi Gras decadence."

Not Too Fancy Bakery

"I went to a French pastry school and fell in love with croissants. That's where that dough comes from."

Calvin Virgil lives in a peaceful, sleepy development in the New Orleans suburb of Kenner. But when you're a home baker and your Carnival creations capture the attention of the region's king cake lovers, it can create awkward moments with your neighbors. "Some days I have a line of people snaking down the block to pick up king cakes," Calvin laughed. "My neighbors wonder, 'What in the world is going on?!'" His king cakes, unique in that they emulate a croissant, are what's going on, and he's developed a loyal following since he began selling them in 2016.

As a child Calvin's passion was savory food.

He remembers his mom and grandmother letting him cut sausage and vegetables or experimenting with seasoning for soul food favorites like gumbo, crawfish bisque, and macaroni and cheese. He joined a culinary club in school and his team advanced to the national championship. "I got stuck with desserts, and at first I was bummed," Calvin recalled, "but that competition was the start of my love for pastries."

Calvin began working in New Orleans restaurants and was awarded a scholarship to New York City's International Culinary Center where he studied pastry making. After graduating, he returned to NOLA and became a pastry cook at Ralph Brennan's Heritage Grill. That's where he invented his king cake. "There was a slow day at work, so I made one and added the candied pecans we had lying around," Calvin remembered. "I drizzled on some caramel, and everyone loved it, so I said let me try to sell it."

His salted caramel candy pecan king cake, with cream cheese filling and white sugar glaze, remains his most popular. Calvin also offers a banana Nutella® king cake and traditional varieties like cream cheese. But it's that croissant dough he uses for all his king cakes that makes them stand out. "I went to a French pastry school and fell in love with croissants. That's where that dough comes from," he said. "It keeps my king cakes from getting too sweet, and it adds a lightness I think people really enjoy."

But what does Calvin think when detractors suggest a croissant dough means it isn't a king cake? "I'd say food evolves over time. Pizzas and pastas have come a long way from their original design, and king cakes have come a long way, too. Why should they suddenly stop evolving now?"

ABOVE: Salted caramel pecan king cake with cream cheese filling and white sugar glaze; **OPPOSITE PAGE:** Traditional king cake with cream cheese filling.

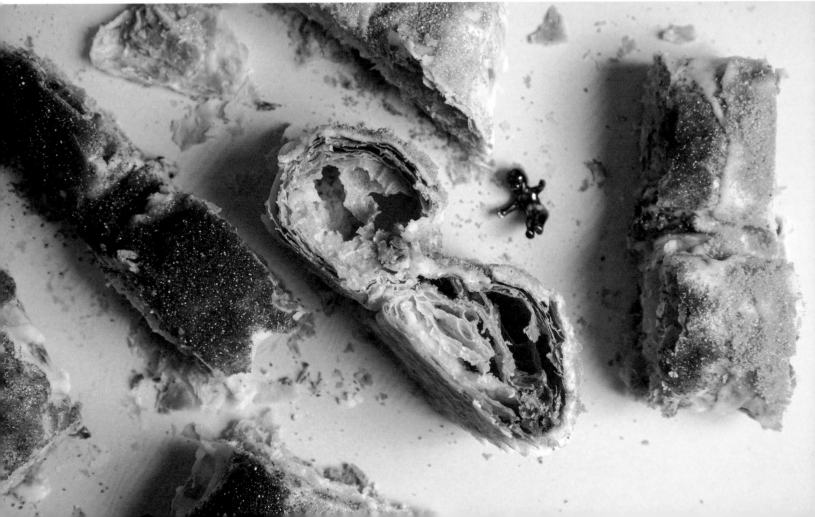

District Donuts. Sliders. Brew.

"It's important to remember king cakes are meant to be shared. If you create this wild flavor that only a few people like, what about everyone else?"

District Donuts has been a must-visit for New Orleans doughnut lovers since they first opened in 2013. The local chain has a knack for grabbing their customers' attention and bringing them back into the store week after week (and sometimes day after day). When unveiling their coveted king cake each Carnival, they apply many of the tricks learned from doughnuts.

For starters, co-owner Chris Audler said, variety is the spice of life. "We have a new slate of donuts each week to keep things fun for our customers," he explained. Similarly, District Donuts creates a new variety of king cake each year. Their first was a doughnut dough twisted and fried. Two later iterations included a king cake modeled after a croissant and even an homage to the colorful Italian fig cucidati cookie. Most recently, they created a cream cheese and dark chocolate king cake reminiscent of cookies and cream.

Another similarity between District's doughnuts and king cakes is the shop's commitment to baking from scratch. Some king cake makers purchase a premade dough, Chris said, but he believes you can taste the difference when the dough comes from fresh ingredients.

But fresh ingredients alone aren't always enough to overcome changing king cake norms. That's led to one important difference in the way District approaches donuts and king cake. "People eat doughnuts the day they buy them," Chris said, "and that's how we used to eat king cake, too." But habits have changed, and customers complain when their day-old cake goes dry. So, Chris' team switched to a croissant dough, helping their king cakes taste fresher longer.

As with doughnuts, Chris is happy getting creative with his king cakes to keep up with changing tastes. In fact, one evolution made Chris a king cake fan in the first place. "I really don't like cinnamon," he said, "and until the late 80s, that's all king cake had." Chris' family got their king cakes from Frances' Bakery (forerunner to Cartozzo's)—one of the first to embrace injecting king cakes with fillings like

  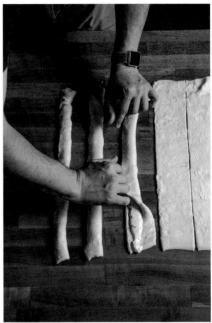

cream cheese, strawberry, or apple like you'd find in a doughnut. "It was really a game-changer for me. The filling overpowered the cinnamon."

While Chris is a fan of filling, he's worried some king cakes might be going too far. "I think it's important to remember that king cakes are meant to be shared with friends and family," he said, "and if you create this wild flavor that only a few people like, what about everyone else at the party?"

And don't get Chris started on one other king cake tradition some bakers have started to eschew. "It's got to be purple, green, and gold," he said. "Please don't mess with the colors!"

OPPOSITE PAGE: Top photo, A pair of cream cheese and dark chocolate king cakes; bottom photo, king cake doughnuts with Carnival-inspired filling.

Brennan's

"Last Carnival we had to order $2,200 worth of pink glitter!"

When it comes to New Orleans dining, particularly fine dining, no family has had a bigger impact than the Brennans. Today, different branches of the famed clan own more than a dozen restaurants.

But it all started with Owen Brennan, the oldest child of six in a working-class, Irish Channel family. In 1943, at just thirty-three years old, he purchased the historic Old Absinthe House on Bourbon Street. His hospitality and gregarious personality turned the bar into such a success, he contemplated adding a restaurant to his portfolio just a few years later.

Legend has it his friend and fellow French Quarter businessman Count Arnaud, owner of legendary Creole restaurant Arnaud's, mocked the idea. He purportedly told Brennan that an Irishman's culinary skills ended with boiled

268

potatoes! Seeing his friend's joke as a challenge, he purchased the restaurant across the street in 1946, calling it Owen Brennan's Vieux Carre Restaurant. Ten years later, it moved into a pink, eighteenth century building on Royal Street. That restaurant—still in the same building and now simply named Brennan's—is celebrating its seventy-fifth anniversary.

Many Creole culinary traditions have been invented in those seventy-five years, including the irresistible Bananas Foster. With so much history, it's surprising king cake is only a recent addition. "They're something we've been talking about making for years," explained baker Patrick Brennan, "but we never had the time or the capacity to actually do it." That capacity finally became available during the coronavirus pandemic shutdown. The result was Brennan's first three king cake varieties.

What's immediately evident is how beautiful the cakes are. The crown jewel of the trio is the strawberry cream cheese king cake, filled with cream cheese and preserves made with fresh strawberries from Johnsdale Farm in nearby Ponchatoula. The preserves, along with pink cocoa butter, gives the icing a pink color that matches the iconic Brennan's building. There's also one more ingredient that gives the cake its pink hue. And it's not a cheap one. "Last Carnival we had to order $2,200 worth of pink glitter," Patrick shook his head with a smile.

PREVIOUS PAGE, LEFT PHOTO: Baker Patrick Brennan (left), Bakery Manager Drew Pope (center), and Corporate Executive Pastry Chef Brett Gauthier in the private Queen's Room at Brennan's. The dress belongs to restaurant co-owner Terry White's daughter, Jane White. Jane was the Queen of Rex in 2011 and this is the incredible eighteen-pound dress she wore, created by Alice Designs Inc. **RIGHT PHOTO:** What goes with a pink cake better than one of New Orleans' most popular dance krewes? Members of The Pussyfooters—in their traditional pink outfits—celebrate their twentieth anniversary with Brennan's strawberry cream cheese king cake.

"Customers often comment on how moist our king cakes are. It's the result of a multi-day Japanese technique called 'tangzhong' that allows the dough to absorb more liquid."

"The other cakes get glitter, too, but the pink is by far the most expensive."

The pink king cake received a lot of well-earned attention in its inaugural year, as did a chocolate "Black and Gold" king cake. But Corporate Executive Pastry Chef Brett Gauthier was insistent they offer a traditional king cake, as well. "We needed a traditional version New Orleanians would love," he said. "Brennan's is known for tradition and quality, and we wanted

our king cake to be viewed similarly."

Nearly all born-and-raised New Orleanians have fond memories of the king cakes they grew up eating each morning during Carnival. For Patrick Brennan, that cake was Randazzo's—and he still tries to get at least one every year. The hope, he said, is that one day, future generations will think of a Brennan's king cake the same way. After all, nostalgia is something the restaurant has excelled at for seventy-five years.

"We have customers in their sixties and seventies, and they say they've been coming to Brennan's since they were ten years old, back when their grandparents used to take them," Patrick said. "More than a half-century later, they're still dining here, but now they're with their grandkids. We love growing traditions. Maybe eating our king cake can be another New Orleanians pass from one generation to the next."

Chapter 7

INTERNATIONAL COUSINS

Louisiana's version of the king cake is unique to the world. The shape, colors, ingredients, taste, and tradition—there's nothing exactly like it. But in large part thanks to the Roman Empire, there are many cakes *kind of* like it.

At the height of its power, Rome extended across the European continent and into the Middle East. But millennia after its geopolitical power receded, the world still feels Rome's legacy in countless ways, including in our language, our infrastructure, and our food. Variations on the king cake and its traditions in places as disparate as Great Britain, Bulgaria, Cyprus, and beyond are examples of that legacy.

As Christianity replaced or adapted many of the pagan elements of ancient Roman customs, king cake was repurposed to commemorate Epiphany and to honor the Three Kings who found the baby Jesus on the twelfth day after his birth. The Spanish called their version the "cake of kings," the Greeks called theirs "king's cake," and the Swiss called theirs "three king's cake," but it's all part of the same Twelfth Night tradition we still enjoy today. Some king cakes are eaten exactly on Twelfth Night, while others are consumed beginning on New Year's. Some are only enjoyed on a specific day of the year, while many, like ours, can be found throughout a season. What they all share, however, is a near-universal use of fruit, nuts, seeds, or sugar for decoration, a round shape, and a charm hidden somewhere inside the cake. The person who finds that symbolic favor is said to be blessed with good fortune and often crowned royalty for the day, or the week, or the season.

This chapter includes some of the most noteworthy relatives to our king cake from across the globe, made by New Orleans locals with ties to those cakes. Some, like the gâteau de rois of southern France or the roscón de reyes of Spain, are our ancestors from which our rituals have directly descended. Others, like the Bulgarian banitsa, are more like cousins, branching off in slightly different ways, but still unmistakably linked to our Louisiana king cake tradition.

Ancient Rome *276*

France *278*

Mexico & Spain *281*

Portugal *282*

England *284*

Switzerland & Germany *286*

Bulgaria *289*

Greece & Cyprus *290*

Ancient Rome: Saturnalia Cake

The Romans celebrated Saturn with a cake, circular like the reborn sun and baked to resemble its golden hue.

Even though, today, king cakes are closely associated with the Catholic holiday of Epiphany, or Twelfth Night, its roots are pagan. In fact, king cake's oldest descendent is believed to be the Saturnalia cake of ancient, pagan Rome. Many of the traditions surrounding present day king cakes—whether French, Spanish, Mexican, or Louisianian—can be traced back to that time.

Each year those early Romans celebrated a winter solstice festival, called Saturnalia, to honor one of their most important gods. The Romans believed Saturn ruled over the world during a Golden Age and, among other things, was the god of agriculture and renewal. Saturnalia was the most raucous feast of the year—simultaneously a marker of the winter harvest, an opportunity for citizens to have fun and fatten up before several final months of frigid weather and food scarcity, and a celebration of the sun's rebirth from its lowest apex in the sky each December 21.

The Romans celebrated with a cake, circular like the reborn sun and baked to resemble its golden hue. A bean was hidden inside and whoever found it in their slice was crowned king or queen for the day. Of course, a monarch during the debaucherous Saturnalia isn't your run-of-the-mill royalty. They were called the "Lord of Misrule" and tasked with creating mischief throughout the festival.

The Saturnalia cake isn't popular in modern day Italy, and the cake's composition is mostly lost to time. Some say it was a galette similar to the galette des rois in France, while most records simply describe it as a round cake sweetened with honey and sometimes stuffed with Roman favorites like figs, dates, and nuts.

While the Saturnalia cake is no longer widely eaten, some parts of Italy do have a Twelfth Night treat with connections to the ancient confectionary. The Befana cake is a dry cake studded with candied fruits similar to a panettone. Like many relatives of the king cake, it's still stuffed with a bean and whoever finds it earns the age-old honor of being queen or king for the day.

The cake is named after Befana, an old innkeeper Italian folklore said hosted the Three Wise Men on their quest to find the baby Jesus. She was such an excellent host she was invited to accompany those Three Kings to meet the son of God. But, ever the martyr, she refused, citing a backlog of housekeeping. That night, it crossed Befana's mind she may have made a mistake. She tried to catch up to the Three Wise Men but was unable. Legend says, to this day, Befana rides her broomstick, still searching for the Christ child and leaving treats (or coal) for the Italian children she passes each Twelfth Night.

The exact composition of a Roman Saturnalia cake is no longer known, but most records describe it as a round cake sweetened with honey and sometimes stuffed with Roman favorites like figs, dates, and nuts. Our version was made by Pastry Chef Alex Hamman, a faculty member in Delgado Community College's culinary arts and hospitality management program.

France: Gâteau des Rois and Galette des Rois

The divergence in cake style is the result of a sixteenth century feud waged between Paris' bakeries and its patisseries.

What began as a wintertime feast cake for the pagans of ancient Rome, was later adopted by Catholics in fourteenth century France. Like the Romans, the French tied the cake to their religion's most significant winter holiday. In the case of French Catholics, that was Epiphany, commemorating the Three Kings finding and presenting gifts to the baby Jesus on the twelfth night after his birth.

The cake wasn't all that made the leap from the Rome of old. So too did the tradition of hiding a fève, or favor, inside it. Originally, that favor was a bean, an ancient symbol for fertility and rebirth. But in the centuries that followed, the Catholic Church replaced pagan symbols with those of their own. The bean gave way to beautifully decorated porcelain fèves, commonly shaped like a miniature crown to represent the Three Kings.

To this day, the French continue the tradition of ordaining the person who finds the hidden favor queen or king for the day. It's a high stakes affair! Children desperately want the honor, while many adults collect the decorative fève. To avoid accusations of cheating, the youngest child— considered the most innocent—is sent under the table. Unable to see which slice has the fève, or which partygoer is up next, they can

assign slices without bias.

Depending on where in France you live, you'll likely find one of two types of king cake. In northern France, there's the galette des rois, made of puff pastry and stuffed with a dense, creamy almond frangipane paste. In the south of France, it's common to find a brioche-style cake, called the gâteau des rois, flavored with cognac or orange blossom. The gâteau has a hole in the center and is covered in candied fruit and granulated sugar— reminiscent of a crown studded with jewels.

The divergence in cake style is the result of a sixteenth century feud waged between Paris' bakeries (specializing in bread) and its patisseries (specializing in cake). The gâteau des rois was proving to be a lucrative Epiphany tradition, and both sides hoped to be granted a monopoly. But when King Francois I ruled in favor of the patisseries, the bakers refused to concede. If they weren't allowed to make the brioche-style king cake, they'd make something that more resembled a king pie. Inspired by the Pithiviers pastry popularized in the Orléans region of northern France, the galette des rois was born!

But both the galette and gâteau faced their toughest test more than two hundred years later when all symbols of the king came under fire during the French Revolution. In 1794, for example, Paris' revolutionary mayor reportedly told his people to, "discover and

OPPOSITE PAGE: Top photo, the galette des rois is most popular in northern France. This galette is from local bakery, La Petite Sophie; bottom-left, a southern French gâteau des rois, also from La Petite Sophie; bottom-right, it's common for French king cakes to come with a creative, hand-painted fève. This galette des rois is from New Orleans' Levee Baking Co.

arrest the criminal patissiers and their filthy orgies which dare to honor the shades of the tyrants!" Revolutionaries pushed for the cake to be outlawed, or at least renamed to the "galette de la liberté" or the "galette de l'egalité" to shift the focus to freedom and equality instead of monarchs. Those names didn't stick, but for a short while, the king cake was referred to as Le Gâteau des Sans-Culottes, which translates to "the Cake of the Men-Without-Pants" in honor of the French revolutionaries. Alternatives to the porcelain crown fève also became popular, and that trend lives on.

Contemporary favors depict works of art, classic movie stars, or even popular cartoon characters. To this day, the French president is served a cake with no fève at all for fear naming a politician king, even for the day, could be dangerous.

The tradition of eating king cake in France was once reserved for Epiphany. Like in Louisiana, that's expanded. Some families enjoy the cake beginning the first Sunday of the year, while others enjoy it throughout January with galette flavors ranging from chocolate to rice pudding and caramel!

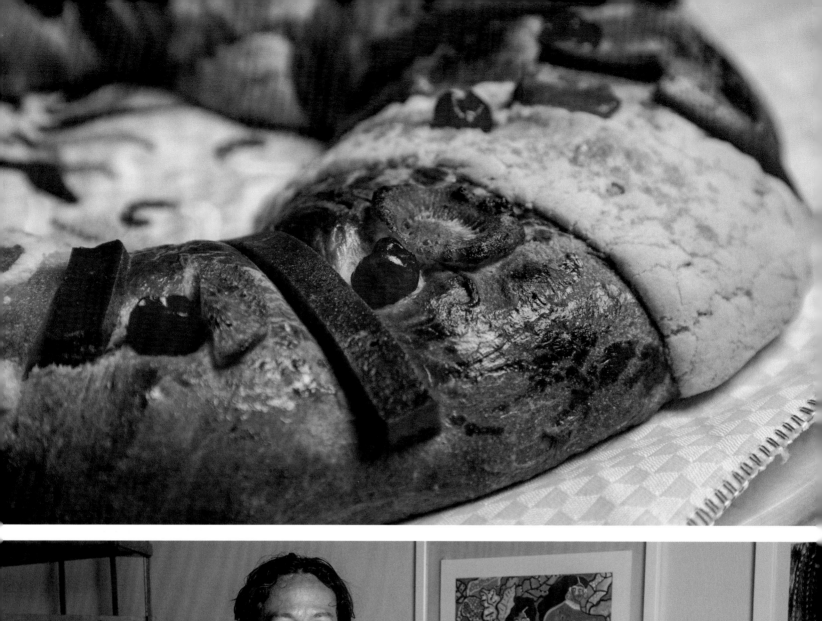

Mexico & Spain: Rosca de Reyes

Depending on where you are, it's called the tortell de reis, the roscón de reyes, or the rosca de reyes, but each time the translation's the same: cake of kings.

The Twelve Days of Christmas are alive and well throughout Spain and much of Latin America. From late December through early January, families throw elaborate holiday feasts that last for hours. While the menu may look a little different depending on the country or family, one constant is that there is always a cake served on January 6. In the Catalonia region of Spain that cake is called the tortell de reis. In the rest of the country, it's the roscón de reyes. In Latin America—especially in Mexico, where it's very popular—they call it the rosca de reyes. In each instance, the translation's the same: cake of kings.

Although there are variations in each version, all are made from a brioche-like dough, similar to what you'd find in southern France and in all Louisiana king cakes until the 1970s. The dough is flavored with orange blossom water or rum and adorned with candied fruit such as cherries,

New Orleans residents Francisco Magallán (left) and Vianey López Amador with their traditional Mexican rosca de reyes. In Mexico, the rosca typically has no filling, but is topped with stripes of sugar paste and candied fruit. Franciso and Vianey own Veggie Tamales, a vegan Mexican food pop-up restaurant in New Orleans.

orange, quince, and figs to resemble a jeweled crown. Fillings can vary from the sweet, whipped cream most popular in Spanish cakes, to less traditional options like chocolate, strawberry, or marzipan. The Mexican rosca de reyes typically has no filling, but stripes of sugar paste join the candied fruit topping.

In countries like Spain and Mexico, Epiphany is one of the most significant days of the Christmastide season. In some ways—especially for children—it's even more important than Christmas Day. While much of the world looks forward to Santa Claus traveling the globe on December 25, Mexican and Spanish families wait for the biblical Three Kings to bring gifts on January 6, just as they did for the Christ child. Their king cake is enjoyed before or after the Epiphany feast; in Mexico it's often served with a cup of hot chocolate.

In Spain, the roscón de reyes includes a bean, as well as a tiny figurine of a king, the baby Jesus, or a figure from pop culture. If you get the bean, you are expected to buy the cake next Twelfth Night. If you find the figurine, however, the prize is much sweeter. You're adorned queen or king for the day and encouraged to wear the paper crown that comes with the cake as a symbol of Your Excellency.

Mexicans hide a baby figure in their cake, symbolic of Mary and Joseph hiding their baby from the persecution of the Roman-backed King Herod of Judea. The partygoer who finds the figurine is expected to host the Día de la Candelaria party on February 2, another important date on the Catholic holiday calendar and related to our Groundhog's Day.

Portugal: Bolo-Rei

Like the Louisiana king cake, this Portuguese equivalent has many similarities to the gâteau de rois of southern France.

Portuguese tradition once dictated Christians should eat a dozen bolos-reis during the twelve days between Christmas and Epiphany. Today, Portugal loves its version of king cake so much, it's available from the start of November all the way through the end of January. It's no wonder, then, that the country's national bakery, Confeitaria Nacional, sells as much as two tons of the cake daily during the season.

Like the Louisiana king cake, this Portuguese equivalent has many similarities to the gâteau de rois of southern France. That's because when the Confeitaria Nacional opened in 1829, the Crown hired a pastry chef from the southern French city of Toulouse. He brought his recipes with him, including one for the Carnival gâteau. Both cakes are round, for example, and made of a soft bread-like dough baked with a large hole in the center to resemble a crown. Raisins, nuts, and crystalized fruit act as the crown's jewels. But shape and toppings aren't all the bolo-rei shares with its cousin in France. When the Portuguese monarchy fell in 1910, the new republic's founders pushed to have the cake renamed so as not to mention the king. Just like in France more than a century earlier, the revolution succeeded but the name-change failed.

Over the years, the bolo-rei diverged slightly from the gâteau. On Epiphany, for example, the cake receives a nougat crown made of caramel and almonds, as well as decorative golden strands created by boiling eggs in a sugar syrup.

Another unique aspect of bolo-rei tradition is that it wasn't only used to determine who will have good luck; it also predicted bad luck. In Portugal, both a charm—such as a small coin—and a fava bean were once baked into the cake (at least before breaking one's tooth became such a concern). The person who found the charm was said to enjoy a year of good luck, while the individual who discovered the bean had to buy the next cake. Sharing the sentiment of many a Louisianian, the Portuguese don't consider buying the next cake a positive thing. As a result, the word "fava" is often used to express bad luck or worse. "Calhou-me a fava!" means "I got the short end of the stick!" while "vai à fava" translates to something too rude to print in this book!

OPPOSITE PAGE: Top photo, fruit and nuts serve as the jewels on the crown-shaped bolo-rei; bottom-left photo, New Orleanian Mariana Rodrigues with her bolo-rei. Mariana is of Portuguese and Brazilian descent; bottom-right photo, in addition to a fava bean, a coin was traditionally hidden inside the Portuguese cake.

England: Twelfth Night Cake

Over time, Twelfth Cake became a rich fruit cake containing brandy, covered in a layer of royal icing, and topped with elaborate, expensive sugar figurines and sculptures.

Aptly named, the Twelfth Night Cake, or Twelfth Cake, was a spiced cake served in England on January 6 to celebrate Epiphany. The date was once the highlight of the twelve-day long Christmastide festival known as the Twelve Days of Christmas. For centuries, Twelfth Night, not Christmas, was the time for gift giving, just as many households in Mexico still do today. The final night was marked by an incredible feast with an elaborately decorated Twelfth Cake as the focal point.

During the medieval and Tudor periods, the cake resembled a yeast-leavened bread, enriched with dried fruit and ale. These were common ingredients among many winter feast cakes, which explains why so many relatives to our king cake contain dried fruit and traces of alcohol. Over time, Twelfth Cake became a rich fruit cake containing brandy, covered in a layer of royal icing, and topped with elaborate, expensive sugar figurines and sculptures. Bakers across Britain would compete to create the most breathtaking cakes.

A dried bean was baked inside the right side of the cake and a pea on the left. Gentlemen were given a slice of cake from the bean-side,

ladies from the pea-side, and whoever found the hidden objects were known as the Lord and Lady of Misrule. It's a name Shakespeare fans may recognize from the play *Twelfth Night*, and history fans may recognize from the Roman Saturnalia festival. During Henry VII's reign, the Lord of Misrule was renamed the Abbot of Unreason—a moniker I've probably earned at an alcohol-fueled festival or two.

Twelfth Cake declined in popularity after the Industrial Revolution. The era's more stringent work requirements made it impossible to celebrate all twelve days of Christmastide. Brits embraced new Christmas traditions during the nineteenth century reign of Queen Victoria, including moving the focus from Epiphany to December 25.

Today, the holiday dessert of choice in most British households is a Christmas pudding. A bit like a fruit cake, each member of the family is told to stir the mix three times and make a wish. If an unmarried person doesn't take part, they are told they won't find a partner in the upcoming year. (Ouch!)

But several more familiar traditions have been carried over from the Twelfth Cake, as well. A coin, and a small crown figurine or silver ring is hidden inside the pudding. If someone finds the coin, they are said to have good fortune. If they find the crown or ring, they are ordained queen or king for the day.

Pastry Chef Alex Hamman, a faculty member in the culinary arts and hospitality management program at Delgado Community College with his Twelfth Night Cake. A bean was commonly hidden inside the elaborately decorated cake. Whoever found it was crowned queen or king for the day.

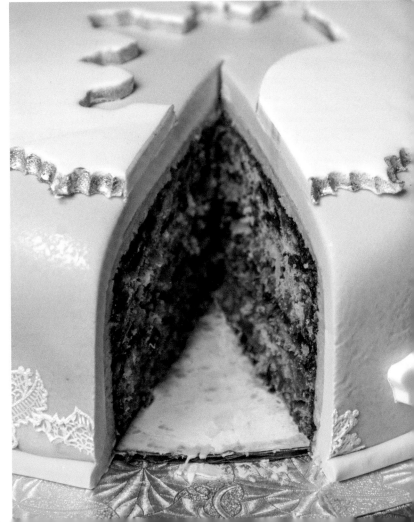

Switzerland & Germany: Dreikönigskuchen

Generally speaking, Dreikönigskuchen is a fluffy, brioche-like cake made of separate rolls arranged in the shape of a crown.

The Dreikönigskuchen dates back to the sixteenth century and translates to English as "Three Kings Cake." The cake—most commonly eaten on Epiphany—is popular in Switzerland and the southern, predominantly Catholic portion of Germany near the Swiss border.

Generally speaking, Dreikönigskuchen is a fluffy, brioche-like cake made of separate rolls arranged in the shape of a crown. Crowns need to be studded, of course, and in Switzerland those jewels are most likely to be in the form of pearl sugar and almond flakes. In Germany, rum-soaked raisins or chocolate chips are often the decoration of choice. The composition of the cake rolls also differs by region. The Swiss version is a sweet bread, while Germans often use a sand batter mixed with dried fruit.

Today, a small, plastic king figurine is frequently baked into one of the rolls, though a plastic baby, almond, pea, or piece of marzipan are also common substitutes. The person lucky enough to receive that special roll is crowned queen or king for the day and receives a crown to wear. It's customary to see Dreikönigskuchens made of eight rolls (plus a larger one filling in the center of the crown), but some bakeries make giant versions with more than fifteen rolls, as well as mini versions with as few as three.

Dreikönigskuchen is also associated with another of the region's popular Epiphany customs. Founded in 1959, Star Singers, or *Sternsinger*, is the tradition in which hundreds of thousands of children go from home to home singing carols and collecting donations for children's aid projects. Just as the king cake is named to honor The Three Kings who traveled through the desert seeking the newborn Christ child, the Star Singers dress as those Three Wise Men for their journey throughout the neighborhood. After singing carols at a home, the children write the year on the door in chalk, along with the initials "C+M+B." The abbreviation stands for "Christus mansionem benedicat," or "Christ bless this house." In return, lucky carolers might receive a roll of freshly baked Dreikönigskuchen. The luckiest will be crowned king or queen.

LEFT PHOTO: Rachel Stickney is the founder of home bakery Sifting in Seersucker as well as a member of the Swiss American Society of New Orleans. She created this Dreikönigskuchen, popular in Switzerland and southern Germany on January 6. **OPPOSITE PAGE:** A small king figurine is commonly hidden inside the cake.

Bulgaria: Banitsa

With the banitsa, everyone's a winner. The branch or messages are placed throughout the cake, so each guest gets a piece of good fortune.

Banitsa is a flaky, savory pastry made of phyllo dough, eggs, yogurt, and the popular Bulgarian sirene cheese. While king cake is connected to the Twelfth Night of Christmas, the banitsa is traditionally enjoyed on the adjacent holidays of Christmas Day and New Year's Eve. Still, many of the customs are related.

Lucky charms, called *kusmeti*, are placed into the pastry. These are often coins or other symbolic objects, such as a small dogwood branch representing health and longevity. Today, many Bulgarians write fortunes on small pieces of paper to be inserted into the cake, predicting—among other things—adventure, a wedding, pregnancy, or education.

The banitsa is cut into as many pieces as there are guests, plus an additional two slices. One of those extra slices is for the house, while the other is for the Virgin Mary, seen as the protector of the family. The pastry is often spun on the table. When it comes to a stop, all guests take the piece in front of them.

And the one with the lucky charm becomes king or queen for the day, right? Wrong! With the banitsa, everyone's a winner. The branch or messages are placed throughout the cake so each guest gets a piece of good fortune. (Unless, for example, you get the "pregnancy" fortune and have no desire to become a parent.)

Banitsa has become ubiquitous in Bulgaria. At all times of the year, street vendors throughout the country sell sweet and savory versions such as spinach, apple, meat, and many more. It's often served at breakfast with a side of yogurt. The crumpled layers of the banitsa's phyllo dough have even earned a prominent place in the Bulgarian lexicon. Today, "banitsa" is used to describe something—mainly documents and paperwork, but also a car in a wreck—that is crumpled, creased, or badly maintained. I beg you not to let your copy of *The Big Book of King Cake* become banitsa.

OPPOSITE PAGE: The banitsa is a traditional holiday treat, enjoyed on Christmas Day and New Year's Eve, and is filled with messages containing fortunes for the following year. Before the messages are inserted into the cake, they are wrapped in tinfoil to be preserved while baking. **RIGHT PHOTO:** This banitsa was made by Bulgarian-American Rali Tiu (right) with the help of her mother, Pavlina Atanasova.

Greece & Cyprus: Vasilopita

This cake from Greece and Cyprus is most closely connected to the New Year, but its relation to king cake traditions is unmistakable.

When the clock strikes twelve on New Year's Day, people across the globe wish each other a happy new year. In Greece and Cyprus they take things up a notch, adding their version of king cake, called vasilopita, to the celebration. The round, flat cake is traditionally sweet to symbolize joy and hope for the new year. It's scented with orange zest and topped with sesame seeds, powdered sugar, and sometimes even the numbers of the year. Depending on the region, some vasilopita are made with yeast and resemble more of a bread than a cake.

But why is vasilopita eaten on January 1 instead of Epiphany? And how did the king cake, most closely associated with Catholicism, arrive in two countries in which only one percent of the population is Catholic?

One clue can be found in the cake's name. Vasilopita (βασιλεύς 'king' + πίτα 'cake'), strongly suggests a connection to the king cakes of Rome and western Europe. Later, a slight reinterpretation resulted in a translation to Basil's cake to honor the life of regionally revered bishop, Saint Basil. In Greece and Cyprus, most traditions and lore surrounding vasilopita have been transferred from the Three Kings to Basil. One example is how they eat the cake on January 1, which also happens to be Saint Basil's Feast Day.

A coin known as a *flouri*, hidden inside the cake, is another opportunity to honor the region's favorite saint. Several countries hide a coin as a fève to symbolize wealth and good fortune, but in the vasilopita, it's once again connected to Basil. One of several legends says that, with his city, Caesarea, under a grueling fourth century siege, Basil asked residents to give him their gold and jewelry to be offered to the invaders as ransom. The attacking army was so moved by the united act of selflessness, they left without the prize. Basil, unsure who to return the riches to, baked them into cakes to distribute around the city. Legend says each citizen miraculously received their exact share back.

Today, the vasilopita still provides an opportunity to receive riches. On midnight of January 1, the head of the household etches three crosses into the cake for good luck. Depending on region and familial traditions, slices are cut for Jesus, the Virgin Mary, the home, the poor, and from the oldest guest to the youngest. Even pets sometimes get a slice. In addition to good luck, whoever finds the coin often receives small gifts. Today, the tradition has spread to businesses and clubs, as well. Those who find the coin during a holiday party can earn prizes so big they put even the Three Kings' gifts to shame.

OPPOSITE PAGE: Top photo, members of the Holy Trinity Greek Orthodox Cathedral Victoria Catsulis (left) and Maria Kyriakides with their vasilopita; bottom-left, some families display the numbers of the new year on top of the cake; bottom-right, sesame seeds are another popular topping. A coin is a common fève to hide inside the vasilopita.

Chapter 8
PUSHING BOUNDARIES

King cake has pushed its own boundaries for centuries, continually expanding the umbrella under which it exists. It was only decades ago, for example, that the introduction of icing caused king cake purists to roll their eyes, and that cream cheese filling was considered eccentric. For a 1985 article in *The Times-Picayune*, baker Louis Klotzbach Jr. of St. Bernard Parish's Klotzbach's Bakery exclaimed, "You wouldn't believe the fillings people ask for: blueberry, blackberry, cream cheese, lemon, pumpkin. Anything you can put in a pie they want in a king cake." Klotzbach said he drew the line at pumpkin, but new residents in the years following Hurricane Katrina (arriving from both within the U.S. and beyond) have helped spawn a new wave of king cake creativity. I wonder how Klotzbach would feel today upon encountering churro king cake and octopus king cake!

Flavor isn't the only king cake boundary being pushed. The late Will Samuels invented the King Cake Hub as a one-stop shop for some of the region's best king cakes. "It's perfect for people who are lazy and don't want to go driving around for hours," Will said during a 2020 episode of the podcast, *Louisiana Eats*. "It's like the Big Easy of king cake shopping."

King cake has gone from a cake not even associated with Carnival to being one of the season's main attractions. The New Orleans Metropolitan Convention and Visitors Bureau estimated in 2019 at least seven hundred and fifty thousand king cakes are sold in the city annually, a number higher than at any other time in history. The cake has become so ubiquitous in recent years that not just one, but two New Orleans sports teams featured king cake-related mascots. The New Orleans Pelicans trot out a giant king cake baby during home games throughout Carnival, while the recently departed New Orleans Baby Cakes minor league baseball team used the imagery year-round.

King cake has reached forms and heights unimaginable even two decades ago. Cricket king cake, king cake classes, king cake for dogs, and more—the innovations of the bakers in this chapter are a big part of both how far king cake has come in recent years as well as where it's going next.

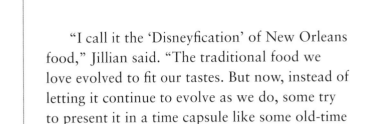

Rahm Haus

"King cake, like most foods, has been evolving long before any of us were alive. Why should it stop now?"

Jillian Duran moved to New Orleans from Long Island in 2013. As a New Yorker, she didn't think much about king cake. But the evolution of a different food type has occupied her mind for years. "I definitely have ideas of what you can and can't call pizza," she said. "Some people say buffalo chicken or Greek salad on a pizza isn't really pizza. But why not?"

She'd ask the same question to someone who believes a king cake can't have boudin, crawfish, or ice cream. "King cake, like most foods, has been evolving long before any of us were alive," Jillian said. "Why should it stop now?" And she has a point. The cream cheese filling we call "traditional" today was radical in the 1980s. The icing and the cinnamon roll dough we now take for granted was new in the 1970s. The purple, green, and gold sugar some say is a requisite of king cake was only added in the last century. The king cakes of two thousand years ago, or even one hundred and fifty years ago would look nothing like what we call "traditional" today.

OPPOSITE PAGE: An onion poppy seed dinner roll dough (without the onions and poppy seeds) is the base for this strawberry malted cream cheese ice cream king cake.
NEXT PAGE: Chef Jillian Duran prepares Rahm Haus' traditionally colored king cake. It features a purple ube dough braided with taro and adzuki bean filling, golden coconut milk ice cream, and green matcha cream cheese frosting.

"I call it the 'Disneyfication' of New Orleans food," Jillian said. "The traditional food we love evolved to fit our tastes. But now, instead of letting it continue to evolve as we do, some try to present it in a time capsule like some old-time food at an amusement park. That's how foods get boring and eventually fade away."

Her argument isn't that "traditional" king cakes should be dismissed. Rather, Jillian believes there's room for both traditional and not. Those who want to push the tradition, she said, should be encouraged. "When people push themselves, there's innovation. The most traditional king cakes of today were products of that."

It's important to note Jillian didn't just roll into New Orleans and begin messing with customs. Her first job after arriving was at Bittersweet Confections, where she learned to make the chocolate king cakes she still considers to be the city's best. When she opened her ice cream shop, Rahm Haus, in 2020, Jillian took what she learned to create innovative, delicious king cakes of her own.

The most popular of her king cakes are stuffed with her Rahm Haus ice cream. The strawberry malted cream cheese ice cream king cake uses an onion poppy seed dinner roll dough (minus the onions and poppy seeds). Her chocolate king cake includes chocolate fluffy dough and black garlic caramel, as well as chocolate ice cream and ganache made in collaboration with Piety and Desire Chocolate. A tri-color ice cream king cake features purple ube dough braided with taro and adzuki bean filling, golden coconut milk ice cream, and green matcha cream cheese frosting.

"Some people go out of their way to tell me, 'Hey! That's not king cake!'" Jillian laughed, "but I want to get even crazier. Why not a pizza king cake next? Or a calzone king cake?"

Jillian thinks the meteoric rise in new king cake varieties is due to the increasing number of pop-up bakers in the city. She doesn't expect that to change any time soon. "In the past you had a handful of big bakeries that signaled, 'This is what king cake is.'" Today, she said that's no longer the case. "There's been a surge of new bakers and we're saying, 'You know what?' we think these versions are king cakes, too!"

This collaboration king cake includes ice cream and ganache made with chocolate from Piety and Desire Chocolate. The base is a chocolate fluffy dough, and the cake is topped with a drizzling of black garlic caramel.

Café Du Bone

"Dogs love us unconditionally, and they deserve our unconditional love back."

The name Denise Indorf chose for her dog-focused bakery and boutique, Café Du Bone, tells us a lot about the Slidell, Louisiana, shop. "It's a riff on the famous Café Du Monde®," she said, referring to New Orleans' beloved beignet and coffee stand. "A lot of what I carry for animals is based on things I've seen us humans love." Her store is full of premium food, clothes, and toys for pets, as well as a full line-up of Denise's creative, homemade dog-centered baked goods.

Canine Cannoli, Beg-nets, and crawfish-flavored snacks are the "norm," while specialty treats like the Pup-Eye's Chicken Biscuit, Port of Bark Burger, Canine Cochon de Lait, and the parmesan-flavored Mama Rover all play off past and present New Orleans culinary institutions. "People love to spoil their dogs," Denise said. "Once a woman ordered a cake for a forty-dog birthday party!"

During Carnival, Café Du Bone ramps that spoiling up a notch with Denise's doggy king cake. The "dough" is a biscuit she makes from whole wheat flour, peanut butter, honey, and vanilla. The icing is yogurt-based, the colored sugar is the same you'd find on any king cake, and the plastic baby is replaced—for obvious reasons—with a tiny, bone-shaped treat. "Kenny Lopez from WGNO ate one once," Denise laughed, referring to the local television reporter, "and he liked it! It's all human-grade ingredients." The shop sells nearly fifteen hundred king cakes each season. Like all Denise's treats, they're also available for shipping.

Due to the length of time it takes for the yogurt icing to melt, a single batch is hours of work. But, for Denise, it's a labor of love. She hosts doggy socials at her shop, and she's the president of the local dog parade, Krewe du Paws. Both are efforts to raise money for rescue shelters like Zeus' Rescues in New Orleans. "I think Zeus' exists for the same reason I opened my shop," she said. "Dogs love us unconditionally, and they deserve our unconditional love back."

LEFT PHOTO: Denise Indorf, owner of Café Du Bone.
OPPOSITE PAGE: A sampling of the four-legged residents at Zeus' Rescues, a New Orleans rescue shelter, enjoying their first bites of king cake. Zeus' has two NOLA Zeus' Place locations, as well, offering grooming, boarding, and daycare services.

Why are King Cakes Round?

There's no mistaking a king cake when you're lucky enough to have one in front of you. But what makes it so distinct? The colored sugars and the taste of sweet icing, cinnamon, and either a brioche or cinnamon roll dough are all clues. But there's another feature of the king cake that's often overlooked: its shape.

The older cousins to the king cake, such as the galette des rois or a Saturnalia cake, were circular. Saturnalia celebrates the sun, so a sun shape makes sense. As the king cake became the centerpiece for larger gatherings over the last two centuries, an oval cake became popular. Ovals, after all, can be elongated and still fit in the oven.

Many have inserted a hole in the middle, creating a ring. Mexico's rosca de reyes, southern France's gâteau des rois, and our Louisiana king cake are just a few examples. Some believe the ring emulates a crown, honoring the Three Kings who visited the baby Jesus on Epiphany. Others say the connected, circular shape represents a desire for unity among the world's Christians.

A third, more involved theory claims the cake remembers the atrocities of King Herod, the Roman client king of Judea. According to the Bible, Herod was informed by soothsayers that a new King of the Jews was born to replace him. The king vowed to kill all Bethlehem children under age two, and when Mary and Joseph fled with Jesus, Herod tracked the Three Wise Men to find the newborn. In this theory, the cake's circular shape emulates the circuitous route the Wise Men took to lose Herod's men.

Or maybe it's just that cakes are often round and the symbology was added later. Like most things steeped in this much history, the only thing we know for sure is that we'll never know for sure.

Audubon Nature Institute

"We chose crickets because they're 'the gateway bug.' They're versatile for cooking and oh so tasty."

Entomology is the branch of zoology dealing with insects, and New Orleanian Zack Lemann is one of the premier entomologists in America. Zack doesn't just study bugs; he cooks and eats them, too, earning him the nickname "The Bug Chef." If you think that's weird, Zack

politely disagrees. "When you consider that we eat crustaceans like crawfish, which are closely related to bugs," he said, smiling, "and that we love honey, which is just nectar regurgitated by a bee, is eating a bug really that wild?"

The Bug Chef can frequently be found cooking up his favorite recipes—everything from chocolate "chirp" cookies and crispy Cajun crickets to elevated cuisine like a dish featuring asparagus and caterpillar—at events across the country and even on *The Tonight Show*. But you're most likely to see him at New Orleans' Audubon Nature Institute where he's worked since 1992. Zack spends most of his time at the Butterfly Garden and Insectarium, home to the popular Bug Appétit Cafe.

Visitors can try more than a half dozen buggy food items any day they visit, but one of the most talked about is only available during Carnival: the cricket king cake. "We chose crickets because they're 'the gateway bug'" Zack said. "They're versatile for cooking and oh so tasty."

Zack isn't the only one who thinks so. During our photo shoot at Audubon Zoo, a live katydid chomped on one of the king cake's crickets. The humans, however, took a little more convincing. One mother offered her skeptical daughter one hundred dollars to eat a slice. (She did.) Another woman watched, interested but from a distance. The Bug Chef, always eager to share the virtues of insect-eating, saw

OPPOSITE PAGE: Survival of the fittest in action as a hungry katydid enjoys its first bite of cricket king cake. (Or maybe just cricket.)

his opening. He talked to her about the health benefits of eating bugs and the cricket's pleasing, nutty flavor. Soon, there was a slice of king cake in her hand. "It's one of the most gratifying things to me," he said afterward. "She was recoiling ten minutes ago, and now she wants a second piece. It's awesome."

Eighty percent of the world's nations already eat insects. Zack's goal is to help Americans discover that bugs can be part of a delicious and healthy diet that's also better for the planet. He knows he has work to do, but living in New Orleans, he said he has a leg up. "If it comes out of a NOLA kitchen, you know it's going to be good, even if it looks a little weird."

LEFT PHOTO: Bug Chef Zack Lemann puts the finishing touches on his cricket king cake. With the Audubon Insectarium in the middle of a move, these photos were taken at Audubon Zoo.

Bearcat Cafe

"I saw baking as my way of adding to this culture I admire so much."

Catalina "Cat" Colby-Pariseau wants to know if there's such a thing as the king cake police. "Do they come around and slap the cake out of your hand and say, 'That's not king cake!'" If such an agency existed, they might take issue with the churro king cake Cat invented for Bearcat Cafe. But Cat says they shouldn't. "I think food is best when chefs can express themselves. Why wouldn't we want people to be creative?"

Hailing from Burlington, Vermont, Cat's aware longtime New Orleanians can be critical of transplants toying with tradition. And she understands why those traditions are valued. "To so many people, that specific, standard type of king cake *is* the tradition," she said. "It's packed with childhood memories." But Cat is sure the city already has enough traditional king cakes. She feels it's okay to add a wrinkle or two as long as the baker comes from a place of respect and knowledge. And she has plenty of both.

Her family, from Quebec, has French roots. When Cat moved to New Orleans eight years ago, she connected with the unique francophone culture and customs of her new home. Her king cake journey began by learning to make the French galette des rois. "Even though king cakes weren't a thing in Quebec," she said, "and my family was more likely to eat meat pies on Mardi Gras, when I moved to New Orleans, I was drawn to the galette."

Baking, in general, was something Cat would explore in earnest upon moving here. She worked as a pastry cook at Kenton's and a pastry chef at Couvant. Her free time was spent reading about baking and trying new recipes, and that hard work paid off. In January 2020, Cat was hired to start a pastry program at Bearcat. "Pastries are such an important thing in places with French influence, and New Orleans has so many amazing bakeries and desserts invented here," she said. "I saw baking as my way to add to this culture I admire so much."

King cake was one way that desire manifested. Cat created a vegan king cake for the vegan-friendly Bearcat Cafe, as well

> *"I think food is best when chefs can express themselves. Why wouldn't we want people to be creative?"*

as her churro king cake, drizzled with dark caramel sauce and modeled after the churro doughnut available there year-round. Some will surely complain this is not a king cake, but—as someone who's never been crazy about churros—I was caught off guard by how much I loved it. That seems to be the consensus among anyone willing to give the churro king cake a chance.

Cat told me it was the city's open-mindedness that brought her back to New Orleans a few years after trying to live elsewhere. "What makes this city so special is how accepting it is," she said. "It encourages you to be unique in a way no other place does. Surely that extends to the way we make king cakes, right?"

Lagniappe Baking Co.

"My first profession was dancing, but I enjoy baking so much, I thought why don't I turn this into a career?"

Kaitlin Guerin's childhood king cake experiences were as traditional as they come. Each week (sometimes twice a week) from King's Day through Mardi Gras, a fellow student's parents would bring a king cake to class, usually plain cinnamon, but sometimes cream cheese. Kaitlin remembers the hidden plastic baby holding significant value. "If you got the baby, you were the coolest kid that day, it was amazing," she said. "You had to bring

the next cake, too, but that was for our parents to figure out." When Kaitlin got home, she'd be greeted by another king cake from Gambino's, Randazzo's, or Adrian's Bakery. "New and fresh, or old and stale, it didn't matter," she said, "I just wanted the icing." Kaitlin laughed remembering the amazing luck she had at home, always finding the baby. "Looking back, I think it was rigged because I was the youngest."

Despite how it must have felt during Carnival, Kaitlin's entire childhood wasn't king cake. She developed a passion for dance and moved to California's Bay Area to pursue that career. But dancing professionally is challenging, and Kaitlin began baking as an outlet for her stress. "I enjoyed it so much," she remembered, thinking, "Why don't I turn this into a career?" She became an assistant pastry chef and enrolled at the Culinary Institute of America at Greystone in Napa Valley.

Her mind now opened to what was possible in baking, Kaitlin returned to New Orleans in 2020 and founded her pop-up business, Lagniappe Baking Co. You can find her at markets, including one at the Hotel Peter and Paul, where she sells homemade pastry boxes with seasonal, local ingredients. "I love pushing the boundaries of my customers' tastes," she said. "I include items that are familiar to lure them in, but then get creative to show how much fun it is to be adventurous and try new things."

OPPOSITE PAGE: In addition to being an accomplished baker, Chef Kaitlin Guerin is a professionally trained dancer. These photos were taken at the Hotel Peter and Paul Church.

"I love pushing the boundaries of my customers' tastes. I include items that are familiar to lure them in, but then get creative to show how much fun it is to be adventurous and try new things."

She employs the same approach with king cake. Both of Kaitlin's cakes are baked with traditional cinnamon and sugar filling, but they're the only king cakes we've found made from homemade sourdough. One of her cakes is a familiar combination of pecan and praline with a hint of rosemary, while the more adventurous variety features candied citrus and chocolate. They're also beautiful, covered in colorful, edible decoration.

Unsure how popular her king cakes would be, she only made twenty that first season. They sold immediately and Kaitlin's considering increasing production for the upcoming Carnival. But she also doesn't mind a more intimate experience. "If my king cake helped two people discover they liked sourdough brioche, then I'm very excited about that."

Kaitlin's view of king cake has come a long way since she was an icing-obsessed child. She's come to appreciate the diversity of options New Orleans' bakers have brought to the tradition. "It's like the city's bakers have put together a curated, edible art walk," she said. "The different cakes speak to each baker's sensibilities and tastes and transform New Orleans each year into a city-wide museum of king cakes. I'm so happy to take part."

TOP PHOTOS: Kaitlin's king cakes are uniquely made with sourdough and topped with beautiful, edible decoration. All photos with Lagniappe Baking Co. were taken at The Elysian Bar, a part of the Hotel Peter and Paul.

Joy The Baker

"I love all the traditions of Mardi Gras and how each person or group creates their own little rituals."

Joy Wilson became Joy The Baker in 2008, though she was a baker (just not *the* baker) before that. While baking goods professionally, she felt a desire to document the food and recipes she was creating on a blog. Fourteen years after starting that blog, she's published three very successful books as well as a seasonal magazine, has a whopping 494,000 Instagram followers, and her blog is now full of

what appears to be infinite recipes. Even though seven of those are king cake recipes, Joy isn't originally from New Orleans. She moved here from Los Angeles in 2013. "I fell in love with the place while visiting," she said, "like so many people do."

Moving to the South hasn't changed Joy's cooking dramatically. "Though, I'm not as afraid of butter and lard," she laughed. The culture, however, is unlike anything she'd experienced before. That's especially true during Carnival. "I love all the traditions of Mardi Gras," she said, "and how each person or group creates their own little rituals." On the Friday before Fat Tuesday, for example, Joy and her friends always go to brunch. During the weekend they meet Uptown for parades. And each day they wear a different costume.

King cake, of course, comes with its own traditions. She remembers the first one she ate, from Haydel's, while visiting a friend. "I found the baby, and I was like what in the world is this?!"

Joy appreciates that there's no bad time to eat a king cake. Like countless New Orleanians, she's snacked on slices in the morning, the afternoon, and at an evening parade. She'll even take the cake home from the parade and eat it again the next morning.

"There's also no bad way to make one!" Joy said. She appreciates a cinnamon roll-style yeast dough king cake just as much as she does a traditional puff pastry galette des rois. On her website she provides, among other king cake recipes, instructions for a cinnamon roll king cake, a biscuit king cake, and even a savory

"*There's no bad way to make one! To me, as long as it has the Carnival colors and a baby, it's king cake, right?*"

smoked sausage king cake. For us, she made a fun pull-apart version, also found on her blog. "To me, as long as it has the Carnival colors and a baby, it's king cake, right?"

Additionally, Joy teaches followers how to make a king cake of their own via one of her popular cooking classes. Last Carnival she taught a virtual class, her most well-attended session yet. It was an opportunity for those non-New Orleans residents to get a taste of Mardi Gras, as well as a chance for locals to practice a skill most have never learned. Despite king cake's ever-growing popularity, they're more likely to be purchased than made at home. Still,

Joy loves giving her followers the opportunity to connect with the baked goods they love. "It's so much fun," she said. "They all send me photos of their progress as they bake along."

Making your first king cake might not go without a hitch, but at the very least, those challenges can help you better appreciate the next king cake you purchase. Joy said, "Sometimes I get a panicked message like, 'Help! What do I do if my king cake exploded!' or something wild like that, but nearly everyone in the class was successful, and they now have this new connection to a really special Carnival tradition."

Que Pasta Nola

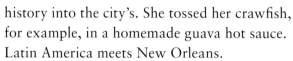

"Something I really appreciate about the United States is all the different cultures here influencing one another. Especially with food."

Anytime someone asks if Amanda Alard's Latin fusion pop-up restaurant Que Pasta Nola is "authentic," she tells them no. "My mom's from Honduras, my dad's from Cuba, I'm from Miami, and my pop-up is in New Orleans," she said. "My food wouldn't be considered traditional in any of those places, but it's inspired by all of them."

Amanda moved here four years ago, and it didn't take long for her to see why her new home was referred to as the northernmost city in the Caribbean. "Cuban food has Creole influences just like New Orleans' and the French Quarter actually looks a lot like Havana." Amanda found the large Honduran population comforting. Hearing whole families converse in Spanish reminded her of home.

"Something I really appreciate about the U.S. is all the different cultures here influencing one another," Amanda said. "Especially with food." That's certainly true in the port city of New Orleans. Amanda began looking for ways her cooking could be inspired by her adopted home's cuisine, as well as ways she could inject her

history into the city's. She tossed her crawfish, for example, in a homemade guava hot sauce. Latin America meets New Orleans.

King cake was another opportunity for Amanda to merge her story with her city's. The first idea was a collaboration with her good friend Chris Nobles from Piety and Desire Chocolate. "We were going to do a Cuban sandwich king cake," she said, "but sadly, someone else was already doing one." Fortunately, the next thought she and Chris had was even better.

It's called the pulpo king cake. Pulpo translates to octopus, a special dish for Amanda growing up. "My aunt cooked it only a few times a year, and I wanted to find a way to make it special for my customers, too." Her solution is to only serve octopus on the eighth of the month ("octo" being the Latin root for eight). Each month is a different dish, but during Carnival, it's king cake time! Amanda's

OPPOSITE PAGE: Que Pasta Nola founder Amanda Alard placing the final octopus tentacle on her pulpo king cake. The king cake is a collaboration with Piety and Desire Chocolate.

king cake octopus preparation involves three days of massaging tentacles, marinating them in a secret family recipe, cooking them sous vide, and searing them.

The black cacao dough, made at Piety and Desire, is a nod to Amanda's feeling that, no matter where she is, she doesn't quite fit in. "She thinks of herself as a black sheep," Chris said. "You can see it in Que Pasta's aesthetics, so the black cacao felt right." The cake's filling is cream cheese and paste from guavas grown on trees in her mother's Miami yard. The topping mixes more of that guava paste with Chris' Hemingway daiquiri ganache, a reference to Amanda's Cuban roots. Even the king cake's familiar cinnamon is mixed with ancho chile and lime for a Latin twist.

The final creation, octopus tentacles reaching out of the cake and into the sky, is unlike anything you've ever seen. And that's exactly how Amanda planned it. "This isn't authentic Honduran food or authentic Cuban food, and it's probably not authentic king cake either," she said, "but it is authentic me. That's what you get at Que Pasta."

A table of patrons at the New Orleans bar, Barrel Proof, dig into the pulpo king cake. The filling and topping include guava paste made from trees in Amanda's mom's Miami yard. Amanda said her mom's guava trees grow so close to mango and coconut trees that her guavas take on hints of those other flavors.

Sugar Love Bakery

"I've always been a creative person, and as a baker in Louisiana, how could I not apply that creativity to king cake?"

Sierra Dee is a king cake entrepreneur. "I've always been a creative person," she said, "and as a baker in Louisiana, how could I not apply that creativity to king cake?"

She remembers when the first idea came to her. "I'm pushing my daughter's stroller around a festival, and everyone is eating chicken on a stick," she laughed. "I thought, 'Couldn't that work on the parade route, too?'" The answer was yes! Since Sierra opened Sugar Love Bakery in 2014, she's sold her King Cake On A Stick to countless Slidell parade goers each Carnival.

King Cake Nuggets were the next innovation ("People wanted fillings in their King Cake On A Stick, so I came up with dipping sauce, instead!") followed by Mardi Gras Hot Chocolate Bombs, a King Cake Charcuterie Board, and even a multi-tiered king cake groom's cake. Outside Carnival season, Sierra creates thematic king cakes to match other holidays. Around Halloween, for example, her "king cake" features a blood-red icing, plastic cleavers sticking out the top, and a green zombie baby.

For someone constantly experimenting with king cakes, it was surprising to learn Sierra didn't have a taste for them growing up.

LEFT PHOTO: Sugar Love Bakery owner Sierra Dee holds up her King Cake On A Stick. **OPPOSITE PAGE:** Sierra also makes king cake groom's cakes for weddings.

"When I baked king cakes at home, my daughter would get into the flour and we'd have these little flour footprints all over the house."

"I didn't enjoy king cake until I started making it myself," she said. More than the taste, Sierra said it was the memories the season created that she loved. "Before I owned the shop, I baked them at home," she smiled. "My baby daughter would get into the flour, and we would have these little flour footprints all over the house."

Sierra hopes her king cake inventions can bring customers joy of their own. "Let all you do be done in love," she said, reciting her favorite Bible verse. "As a baker, that's our job. To find new, creative ways to make our customers happy— one sweet at a time."

TOP PHOTOS: When you pour hot milk on the Mardi Gras Hot Chocolate Bomb marshmallows explode from inside. Lucky customers may also find a plastic baby figure. **LEFT PHOTO:** King Cake Nuggets with a variety of dipping sauces. **OPPOSITE PAGE, TOP PHOTO:** Sugar Love Bakery also makes more traditional king cakes such as this Chantilly cream king cake. **OPPOSITE PAGE, BOTTOM PHOTO:** During holidays outside of Carnival, Sierra makes thematic versions of her king cake. This Halloween king cake features a green zombie baby.

The Station Coffee Shop & Bakery

"There are already people who make traditional king cakes so well, so why am I going to recreate that in my bakery? I'd rather make something new."

At The Station Coffee Shop & Bakery, Megan Walker will wow you with her creativity. A strawberry balsamic king cake, a savory muffuletta king cake, and a coconut cream king cake were three of the varieties she offered last Carnival. Her favorite, however, was based on the kouign amann, the buttery, multi-layered cake *The New York Times* called "the fattiest pastry in all of Europe." The layers are created as the salted butter puffs up the dough, resembling a denser, caramelized croissant. She calls this cake her kouign cake (appropriately pronounced "queen cake").

Though Megan acknowledged king cake preferences vary greatly, she's committed to creating cakes that suit her tastes. "I don't love the sugar bombs," she said. "You know, the ones covered with glaze and sanding sugar. I know people love them, but I just don't." Instead, Megan prefers the bready-brioche dough from

those cakes she enjoyed at her school's weekly Carnival king cake parties. She also adds cinnamon sugar to her kouign cake because, to her, cinnamon *is* the taste of Mardi Gras.

Another of Megan's king cake beliefs is that even though the variety has exploded over the last decade, she believes there's always room for more. And it's not because she can't do traditional. Megan's been baking since she was a kid, getting her start at Angelo Brocato when she was still a teenager. "With traditional king cakes, it's kind of like New Orleans-style French bread," she said. "There are already people here who do those things so well, so why am I going to recreate that in my bakery? I'd rather make something new."

OPPOSITE PAGE: A slice of kouign cake (pronounced "queen cake"); **RIGHT PHOTO:** Megan Walker with her strawberry balsamic king cake (left) and kouign cake (right).

> *"I don't love the sugar bombs. You know, the king cakes covered with glaze and sanding sugar. I know people love them, but I just don't."*

She's been doing just that for almost a decade. In 2012, she began baking out of her Mid-City home. Megan wanted to use flavors traditionally New Orleans, but not traditionally found in king cake. That included savory options. Crawfish and goat cheese, as well as red beans and rice, were two of her early hits.

After Megan met her now-husband Jonathan in a kickball league, they had the idea to merge her baking skills with his coffee expertise. "We fell in love with this beautiful building down the street from our house," Jonathan said. "It took a couple of years to convince the owner to sell it, but he finally did. We love the space, but we really love the idea of serving our neighbors."

Their shop is as quaint a location as you'll find in New Orleans, with a steeply pitched roof and scattered seats among a garden in the front. Stop in and you're likely to see Megan, Jonathan, and maybe even their newborn baby. But, if they're not there, don't worry. Megan laughed, "We're just down the street."

TOP-LEFT PHOTO: Megan Walker drizzles balsamic glaze on her strawberry balsamic king cake. **TOP-RIGHT PHOTO:** Co-owners Megan and Jonathan take a break to enjoy king cake and coffee.

Éclair Délicieux

"They taught us to 'bake to inspire,' and I try to remember that in everything I do."

The months she spent at The French Pastry School in Chicago were some of the most formative of Patty Dinh's life. But those months didn't start smoothly. At her welcome orientation Patty was asked, in front of two hundred students, what brought her to the school. "I told them I was from New Orleans and wanted to create the world's best king cake," she said. "And then they laughed because I guess they thought I was joking or being too ambitious, but I was serious!" Things got worse. On the first day of class, students were given a backpack full of valuable kitchen utensils and knives. "I lost my pack that same day!" Patty said. "I was a mess."

The road to pastry school was a winding one for Patty, who was unsure what career path to pursue. She tried nursing school but struggled to retain information she didn't find interesting. Peace Corps was an option, too, but Patty instead found work as a saleswoman for a home alarm company. "It was something I was actually great at," she said. "It took interpersonal skills and resourcefulness, both of which I think are my strengths."

Patty's resourcefulness was on full display in pastry school. "I went to Chicago partly because I knew if things went badly, I had a friend nearby whose couch I could crash on," she said. It didn't come to that, but money was tight. The eighteen-month program was split into two-week units. Two weeks of pastries, for example, followed by two weeks of pies, then chocolate candies, then ice cream. "We were allowed to take home some of everything we made," she said. "So I basically only ate cake for two weeks before moving on to the next sweet."

LEFT PHOTO: Patty Dinh eyes her beautiful Napoleon king cake.
OPPOSITE PAGE: Top photo, Éclair Délicieux's Napoleon king cake tastes like a Napoleon pastry. The cake is a glazed puff pastry, and the filling is custard mousse. Adding Chantilly cream lightens the taste; bottom photo, one of Patty's specialties is crepe cake, which she began making after her young son got excited by videos of them on YouTube. She offers several varieties. During Carnival, that includes a Mardi Gras version, filled with custard mousse mixed with toasted pistachios and topped with Chantilly cream.

Despite the challenges, Patty recommends pastry school to anyone interested in a baking career. "Our instructors were world champion pastry chefs, and the students were a mix of professionals from around the world and kids right out of high school. It's really an experience for anyone passionate about baking." And Patty fit the bill. After graduating from the program, she returned to New Orleans to start her own shop. First, she went back to work selling alarms, saving money to go toward her business. By the time she'd saved enough, she was expecting a child. That didn't stop her, though. "I was in my last trimester painting and tiling my bakery." Two months after giving birth to her daughter, Éclair Délicieux was finally open.

You can taste Patty's training in the quality of Éclair Délicieux's baked goods, but that's not the only way The French Pastry School has had a lasting impact on her. "They taught us to 'bake

to inspire,'" Patty said, "and I try to remember that in everything I do." Patty inspires visitors with her fun, chic, photogenic bakery, as well as her friendly, encouraging demeanor. She offers a rotating slate of delicious, often-stunning baked goods as well as baking classes to teach dozens of students how to make macarons, eclairs, and Napoleons of their own. "I want people to be in awe of how beautiful pastries can be."

Her Carnival creations do exactly that. In addition to a gorgeous Mardi Gras crepe cake, Patty offers a king cake based on a Napoleon, including the glazed puff pastry and custard mousse filling. She adds mascarpone-based Chantilly cream for lightness, plus colored sugar and fruit to resemble a Chantilly-style king cake. It's some of the best king cake you'll find, particularly if you love Napoleon pastries. "I should hope so," Patty laughed, "I told my classmates I'd make the best!"

King and Queen for the Day

The traditions of Carnival season are packed with allusions to royalty. Mardi Gras krewes crown queens and kings who ride on floats, throwing beads and coins to the masses in the streets hoping for a glimpse of their monarch. The season itself begins on January 6, a day sometimes referred to as Kings Day. And, of course, we eat king cake, often shaped like a crown. The person who finds the baby in their slice becomes king or queen for the day. But where do the traditions come from and what do they get you besides the inconvenience of having to buy your office breakroom's next king cake? Many of these traditions are connected to the story of the Three Kings who found the Christ child on the twelfth day after his birth. But there's a thread between winter holidays and royalty that can be traced back long before that. Around 2,600 BC, the ancient Babylonians celebrated the winter solstice festival of Zagmuk. Peasants were chosen to be mock kings and queens, and all were encouraged to dress as if belonging to social classes other than their own. This is an important point. It's not just that a queen or king is chosen, it's that the strict societal rules of hierarchy are temporarily disrupted.

These customs continued in early Rome, one of the first societies to choose their mock royalty via a cake. During their Saturnalia festival, the individual who found the bean wasn't crowned any old king or queen, but rather, the Lord of Misrule. The Lord was responsible for creating debauchery such as insulting guests, ordering them to do silly things, wearing crazy clothing, and planning scandalous entertainment. (In the earliest festivals, the Lord of Misrule was also sacrificed to the gods, so the next time you complain about having to buy another king cake, exercise some perspective.)

The Lord of Misrule wasn't the only example of flipping hierarchy during Saturnalia. The poor and enslaved were encouraged to participate, as well. They were often given fine garments to wear, sat at the head of the table, and presented with gifts by the wealthy. But why?

These older societies were notoriously rigid. If you were born poor, it was unlikely you'd ever be anything but. It was a tough life, and the weeks after the winter solstice were among the toughest. It was cold, the nights were long, and this final feast before a season of food scarcity was an important time to celebrate and unwind.

We do the same today. When you eat a slice of king cake, find the lucky fève, or ride masked in a parade, you're taking part in the thousands-year-old tradition of temporarily throwing society's often inflexible hierarchy out the window.

Chapter 9

KING CAKE?

It's easy to look at the most adventurous king cakes of the present day and say, "Hey, that's not king cake!" But king cake's evolution is nothing new. If a soldier from the Roman Empire had a time machine to visit thirteenth century Paris, he may have viewed the early galette des rois in the same way you view a sushi king cake. If a thirteenth century Parisian dropped into the 1870s to witness the annual Carnival ball of New Orleans' Twelfth Night Revelers, the fondant-covered "king's cake" would be unrecognizable. And if one of those Twelfth Night Revelers managed to survive until the 1980s, they'd probably have an angry thing or two to say about a brioche cake covered in icing and purple, green, and gold sugar.

Don't get me wrong. I believe tradition is important and learning about centuries of king cake history and customs has been a delight. But what about that tradition keeps it so relevant? Is it really about what dough is used and whether that dough is braided? Is it about the tiny favor hidden inside, or about the ritual that the person who finds that favor receives some good fortune like kingship for a day?

Or is it that the cake, and the favor, and the tradition bring family, friends, bakers, neighbors, and strangers together in celebration? I can't answer for everyone, but for me, that is what I love about king cake.

The "king cakes" in this final chapter are in many ways unique from the ones we're used to seeing. But instead of immediately dismissing them as "not really a king cake," I'd encourage you to consider what makes them similar to the ones you think of as traditional. It's possible in twenty years, a taco king cake will be as common as the cream cheese-filled variety is today. Or maybe it won't. Either way, the creations featured on the following pages are delicious, and they incorporate at least some of the cake's traditional elements, including its shape, a fève, or certain flavors. Whether that makes this a look into the future of king cake, or just a strange and wild detour, will be for future generations of New Orleanians to decide.

Rock-n-Sake

"I love the tradition of sushi, but I also want to be original."

Rock-n-Sake Co-Owner and Executive Chef Dirk Dantin is built like a college athlete, which makes sense because he was a hall of fame baseball player at local Loyola University. He's since retired, but a competitive fire still burns within him, and you can see that fire in his sushi king cake.

"I love the tradition of sushi," Dirk said, "but I also want to be original." Originality isn't easy when a food's existed for millennia, but that didn't stop Dirk from relentlessly brainstorming. One morning the idea he'd been waiting for came to him. "I said 'I'm going to make a *&@%^&# king cake!'"

Executing the idea took experimentation. The biggest challenge was getting the rice base to hold together in a curvilinear shape. The solution was a traditional Japanese technique called hako-zushi, or box sushi. In this method, Dirk presses his layers of rice, cream cheese, snow crab salad, and more rice into shape with a box-like mold. He then uses his hands to gently curve the edge into the traditional king cake ring.

To emulate the colorful look of a king cake, Dirk tops the pressed creation with alternating sections of tuna, salmon, yellow tail, spicy tuna, and avocado, and switches between garnishes like lime, jalapeno, lemon zest, and green onions. "If you love sushi," Dirk said, "you're going to love this."

To order the sushi king cake, you'll need to call one of his three Rock-n-Sake locations on Old Metairie Road, in Baton Rouge, or in Lafayette at least twenty-four hours in advance. But Dirk's sure you'll be glad you did, as will the friends you share it with. "If you walk into your king cake party with a sushi cake, you're going to get some smiles," he said. "It's unique, and that's exactly what I set out to create."

RIGHT PHOTO: Dirk Dantin constructs his sushi king cake. Dirk said customers are welcomed to customize their cake if there are certain types of fish they prefer.

341

Bakery Bar

"Calling it king cake doberge will get us in trouble with the purists. We like to call it king cake-flavored doberge."

Bakery Bar co-owners (and sweethearts) Charlotte McGehee and Charles Mary IV are known for their doberge cake, the local dessert built with seven layers of cake and six layers of pudding. Created by Beulah Ledner nearly a century ago, it's an adaptation of the Hungarian dobos torte made lighter to better complement the muggy Louisiana weather.

Charlotte's love affair with southeast Louisiana's second most famous cake began when she was hired at a bakery in Baton Rouge. The newest employee, she was given the "honor" of stacking the cake's many layers. "It's tedious work nobody else wanted," she said, "but I happened to enjoy it." Years later, after moving to New Orleans, Charlotte was telling friends about her experience

with doberge. Impressed, they encouraged her to create a pop-up bakery. Charlotte did exactly that, under the name Debbie Does Doberge, a reference to the classic 1978, uh, film.

After the pop-up's success, Charlotte and Charles opened Bakery Bar, a bakery-slash-bar-slash-full service restaurant, as well as their newest bakery and cocktail bar, Debbie on the Levee.

Over the years, the duo has sold more than fifty flavors of doberge. Each Carnival, that includes their Mardi Gras doberge cake, featuring ingredients commonly associated with king cake such as cinnamon, cream cheese, and purple, green, and gold sugar. So, is it a king cake doberge? "Whoa whoa, whoa, that's going to get us in hot water with purists," Charlotte laughed. "We like to call it king cake-*flavored* doberge."

Their prudence isn't just lip service. The pair, both born and raised in Louisiana, have a strong respect for king cake etiquette.

"There are rules to abide by," Charles explained. "First, if you get the baby in your slice, you don't try to sneak it back in the dough, you buy the next cake. Second, the king cake knife always stays in the box until the cake is finished. Third, putting a dry king cake in the microwave for fifteen seconds will return it to its former moist glory. And—the most important rule—it's Carnival, so do what you wanna!"

You heard him. Do what you wanna. Even if that means occasionally forgoing a king cake for a king cake dob—I mean a king cake-*flavored* doberge!

TOP PHOTO: In addition to the Mardi Gras doberge cake (previous page, with co-owner Charlotte McGehee), Bakery Bar makes colorful king cake beignets. **OPPOSITE PAGE:** Bakery Bar manager Vincent Heitz teaches us how to make two Carnival-themed cocktails.

King Cake Martini

Mix the following ingredients in a shaker

> 1½ oz Vodka
> ¾ oz Cinnamon syrup
> ¾ oz Cream
> ½ oz Orgeat

- Add ice

- Run a lemon wedge around the rim of a coupe glass

- Press rim of glass onto a plate containing purple, green, and gold sugar

- Shake the ingredients in shaker and double strain into coupe

- Top with grated cinnamon and garnish with plastic baby

Mardi Gras Sazerac

Mix the following ingredients in a stirring glass

> 2 oz Sazerac rye
> ½ oz Cinnamon syrup
> 2 Dashes Peychaud's Bitters
> 1 Dash Angostura® Bitters

- Add ice

- Stir thoroughly

- Run a lemon wedge around the rim of a rocks glass

- Press rim of glass onto a plate containing purple, green, and gold sugar

- Spritz glass with vanilla liquor

- Strain contents of stirring glass into rocks glass

- Garnish with orange peel

Bratz Y'all!

"In Berlin, on Fat Tuesday, it's tradition to buy jelly doughnuts to eat with our friends. Except, we like to trick them by filling some doughnuts with mustard. They have no idea until they take a bite!"

"**S**ometimes people come up to me, point to our king cake pretzel, and say, 'Hey Sven, that's not king cake!' and I say, 'Yeah, I know. That's why we call it a king cake *pretzel*!'"

Sven Vorkauf had a thousand stories to tell in his thick Berlin accent as he tossed newly shaped pretzels into the oven. He told me how he first arrived in New Orleans. (He was on a vacation in Fiji and some New Orleanians told him he *had* to visit.) He told me why it's fitting that his German beer garden, Bratz Y'all, is in the Bywater. (German immigrants were among the neighborhood's earliest settlers.) And he told me why he hides a walnut instead of a baby in his king cake pretzel. "I thought maybe it's not smart to bake plastic into a pretzel." But is the walnut symbolic in Germany? "No, but I like them and they're good for the brain. So, if you get the walnut, it's a no brainer—buy another king cake pretzel!"

Sven said Carnival is celebrated in the predominately Catholic southern part of Germany, but not in Berlin. The extent of northern Germany's revelry is eating the donut-esque, jelly-filled Berliners on Fat Tuesday with friends and family—a nod to the older tradition of eating decadent foods the day before Lent.

In New Orleans he wanted to take part in the festivities in a way that felt true to his restaurant. Bratz Y'all makes what are widely considered the city's best pretzels, so that seemed a good place to start. "A Bavarian pretzel filled with Bavarian cream and covered in Carnival colors," he said. "It's the perfect match, but don't get mad at me if you don't think it's king cake!"

LEFT PHOTO: Sven Vorkauf in the courtyard of Bratz Y'all with a beer and his king cake pretzel. The pretzel is sliced in half and filled with Bavarian cream.

Casa Borrega

"Suddenly, New Orleans felt more familiar. This was a tradition I recognized."

The first time I saw Casa Borrega's taco king cake was in 2017. Rather than a king cake filled with taco ingredients like one might expect, I was surprised to find a series of individual tacos arranged in the king cake's familiar, elliptical shape. Some tacos were filled with carnitas, some with chorizo, some with chicken and others with picadillo. To create the Carnival colors, yellow pineapple, purple onions, and green cilantro were added, as well as a generous helping of plastic baby fèves for good measure. Limes and several colorful sauces were placed on the platter. It was a beautiful dish, but was it really king cake? Or was this just a glorified taco platter meant to profit off a growing king cake mania?

To understand the taco king cake, you must understand that to Casa Borrega owner Hugo Montero, king cake is more than just a cake. Like a New Orleanian talking about their first king cake from McKenzie's or Randazzo's, Hugo remembers his childhood rosca de reyes with fondness. "We looked forward to January 6 so much," he said. "The day is bigger than Christmas in Mexico. Santa Claus is more of an Anglo-Saxon tradition, but January 6 is the day the Three Wise Men brought us presents. And it's the only day in Mexico we eat rosca de reyes."

Hugo moved to New Orleans more than thirty years ago. It was a new, strange place. The unfamiliarity sometimes made him homesick. But that feeling subsided somewhat as his family grew. Hugo soon had two American-born sons, which meant his story was now forever tied to his new home.

His children grew up loving the things most American kids loved. In New Orleans, that of course meant Carnival. "I'll never forget the day I took my kids into the McKenzie's bakery on Canal Street," Hugo said. "When my youngest saw king cake for the first time, his eyes got so big, it touched me, because I imagine that's how

LEFT PHOTO: Casa Borrega owner Hugo Montero (right) and the restaurant's main cook Daisy Xiomara Cruz with their taco king cake.

my eyes looked when my parents brought in the rosca de reyes. Suddenly, New Orleans felt more familiar. This was a tradition I recognized."

Hugo says he's impressed with his adopted city's obsession with king cake. "Some cultures have Carnival, but they don't have king cake. Others have king cake for just a day, but not everyone participates. But in New Orleans, it's a way of life."

When he founded Casa Borrega, Hugo wanted to add a Mexican representative to the city's slate of king cakes. The problem was he didn't have the equipment to bake on a large enough scale. One day while shopping, he found his solution. He saw an oval platter that reminded him of a king cake. He invented his taco king cake that day. The reasons were obvious to him. "I wanted to pay homage to something important to my new home, and also integral to my past. Plus, who doesn't love tacos?"

TOP PHOTO: Team members at Casa Borrega prepare the tacos for their unique king cake. **BOTTOM PHOTO:** Educators from nearby school KIPP Central City Academy enjoy the king cake during happy hour.

Jack Rose

"This was my first job I had the freedom to create my own desserts, but the one I quickly learned was non-negotiable was the Mile High Pie."

King cake isn't the only cake in New Orleans with history, said Eka Soenarko, executive pastry chef at the Pontchartrain Hotel's restaurant, Jack Rose. "Guests came to our hotel decades ago with their grandparents to eat our Mile High Pie. All these years later, they're back to share it with their grandchildren."

The Pontchartrain Hotel opened in 1927, attracting scores of celebrities and American presidents over the years. In 1948, the Caribbean Room restaurant was added, led by the influential Chef Nathaniel Burton. Described as being "to the skillet what Louis Armstrong was to the trumpet," Burton was the inventor of the Mile High Pie. It consisted of four layers of vanilla, chocolate, strawberry, and peppermint ice creams, surrounded by scorched meringue and topped with chocolate sauce.

The iconic dessert is still offered today at the Caribbean Room's successor, Jack Rose. Now it's Eka who oversees its production. She moved to New Orleans from Indonesia in 2006. After long stints at the Windsor Court and the Hyatt Regency ("where I had to make so many king cakes!"), she was recruited to Jack Rose in 2019. "This was my first job I had the freedom to create my own desserts," she said, "but the one I quickly learned was non-negotiable was the Mile High Pie."

Restaurants in New Orleans often concoct something special for the Carnival season. In 2020, Eka and her team created Mardi Gras-themed donuts. The next year, with parades cancelled, they decided to go bigger. "My favorite thing about Carnival is that everyone can be both the entertained and the entertainer," she said. "Jack Rose is on the parade route, and we thought we could add some joy to a unique Carnival." Their solution was the Mile High Mardi Gras Pie.

RIGHT PHOTO: Executive Pastry Chef Eka Soenarko with her Mile High Mardi Gras Pie.

It took trial and error as the team brainstormed flavors to transform their classic dessert into something king cake colored. Blueberries and purple potatoes, for example, were originally considered for purple. In the end they decided on ube for purple, mango for gold, and pistachio for green. "We don't use food coloring, so that means we go to nearly every Asian market in the area finding enough ube to make that vibrant purple," Eka said. The dessert is served with a coconut-cornflake crumble for texture and topped with scorched meringue, chocolate sauce, and a sparkler for good measure.

The Mile High Mardi Gras Pie was a big success, with at least one hundred and twenty sold each week last Carnival. The cake-making process takes three days, so it's a busy time for the pastry team at Jack Rose. But Eka doesn't regret it. "It's busy, sure, but this is our homage to two famous New Orleans cakes and the Carnival season. It's worth the extra effort!"

Copeland's of New Orleans

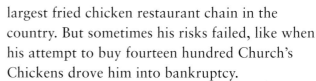

"Nobody celebrated Mardi Gras and New Orleans like Grandpa."

The Mardi Gras cheesecake is a nod to the larger-than-life Al Copeland, Sr., founder of restaurant concepts like Popeyes fast food chicken, Copeland's of New Orleans, and countless others. In a 2008 article after his death, *The New York Times* referred to Al, Sr. in the same way *The Times-Picayune* once had—as "Louisiana's homegrown Liberace." But that's not how his life began. Al was raised by a single mother, at times in a public housing project. He never finished high school, but he was an entrepreneur from an early age. He bought a Tastee Donuts franchise when he was just eighteen years old and created the original Popeyes a decade later in 1972.

Al was known for taking risks. "Vegas was his second home," laughed his granddaughter, Allison Copeland Donnelly, vice president of Al Copeland Investments. Sometimes those risks panned out. Popeyes grew to eight hundred locations under Al's watch, becoming the third-largest fried chicken restaurant chain in the country. But sometimes his risks failed, like when his attempt to buy fourteen hundred Church's Chickens drove him into bankruptcy.

Equally as famous as Al's work inside his restaurants was his lavishness outside them. He raced speedboats, collected cars, and had four elaborate weddings that—depending on the marriage—featured heart-shaped fireworks, a snow machine, ten thousand white roses, and the transformation of his Metairie mansion into a Disney castle. Even his philanthropy was opulent. In addition to establishing an endowment in his name at Louisiana State University, each holiday season he'd provide gifts for thousands of at-risk children and turn his previously mentioned mansion into one of the most spectacular Christmas light shows in the country.

It's no surprise that a New Orleanian this flamboyant loved Mardi Gras. "Nobody celebrated Mardi Gras and New Orleans like Grandpa," Allison said, remembering how each year he'd convert one of his boats into a float for the family to parade on.

The company is now run by Al's son, Al Copeland, Jr., and Allison said they still try to honor their former patriarch's legacy. "Whether it's continuing his philanthropy with The Al Copeland Foundation, tapping into his decadence with our wild Crash and Burn cocktail, or honoring his love for Mardi Gras with our seasonal cheesecake, we try to run our company the way he lived."

LEFT PHOTO: Three sisters Ariel (left), Alexandria (middle), and Allison are granddaughters of Al Copeland, Sr. and have careers in the family business.

Creole Creamery

"Those king cake flavors are as much a part of this building and of New Orleans history as the McKenzie's sign out front."

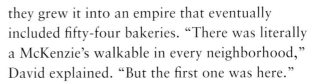

The king cakes chosen for this book were usually the best that location had to offer. That's no different with the ice cream king cake at Creole Creamery: eight scoops of house-made king cake ice cream covered in an additional softened layer of ice cream—this one a cinnamon-vanilla flavor dyed purple, green, and gold. It's not a "cake" per se, but it includes chunks of Danish dough, and the whole creation is topped with Carnival-colored sprinkles and cherries. It's likely the most delicious king cake ever made at 4924 Prytania Street, but it's not the most famous.

Creole Creamery Owner David Bergeron doesn't take that as an insult. "Our shop is in the very first McKenzie's store," he said. "It's basically where the modern Louisiana king cake was invented!"

McKenzie's Pastry Shoppes was founded in 1929 (originally a few doors down before it moved to this location) by Henry McKenzie. When the Entringer family purchased it in 1936,

they grew it into an empire that eventually included fifty-four bakeries. "There was literally a McKenzie's walkable in every neighborhood," David explained. "But the first one was here."

He sees it as his responsibility to care for the building in which not only the king cake was popularized, but also the plastic baby figurine we hide inside them. "We New Orleanians are great at tradition," he said. "Families live here for generations, so we pass our rituals down to our kids."

Case in point, David still remembers eating king cake as a child (from McKenzie's of course) at his grandmother's table each year. "That's still what king cake is to me. It's nostalgia and it's family," he said. And just as he cares for his famous building, he thinks it's equally important to care for our traditions. "Customers ask me if I'll make the ice cream king cake with different flavors, and I say no way. Those king cake flavors are as much a part of this building and of New Orleans history as the McKenzie's sign out front."

But David's no king cake purist. He knows an ice cream king cake isn't traditional, and he looks forward to trying the craziest flavored king cakes each year. But this duality needn't be irreconcilable, he said. "Can't I appreciate creativity and stay connected to my past? Even if it's only in the flavor of my ice cream, can't I do both?"

McKenzie's Pastry Shoppes once had fifty-four locations around New Orleans. The first location was at what is now the Creole Creamery on Prytania Street. The old McKenzie's sign still sits atop the shop's entrance.

King Cake Mania

From food and alcohol to clothing and jewelry, king cake's influence has expanded to items that can't possibly be considered a king cake, or a cake at all, or sometimes edible for that matter! We hear, for example, there's a very nice king cake coffee table book out there. The list grows every year, but here are just a few of the many king cake-inspired items you can find around New Orleans.

1. King Cake Soap from Green Oaks Apothecary. **2.** King Cake Popcorn from Cajun Pop. **3.** King Cake Donuts from Rickey Meche's Donut King. **4.** King Cake Krewe of Muses signature shoe "throw" by krewe member Nori Pritchard, co-owner of NOLA Craft Culture. **5.** King Cake Milkshake Sour beer from Urban South Brewery. **6.** King Cake Charcuterie from Sugar Love Bakery. **7.** King Cake Affogato with king cake-flavored ice cream from Creole Creamery. **8.** King Cake Macarons from Violet Sprinkles. **9.** King Cake Rum Cream from Joe Gambino's Bakery and Cocktail & Sons. **10.** King Cake ice cream (and Mardi Gras Pie ice cream) from New Orleans Ice Cream Company. **11.** King Cake Earrings from Pete's Papercrafts presented on a purple, green & gold Carnival cutting board from NOLA BOARDS.

362

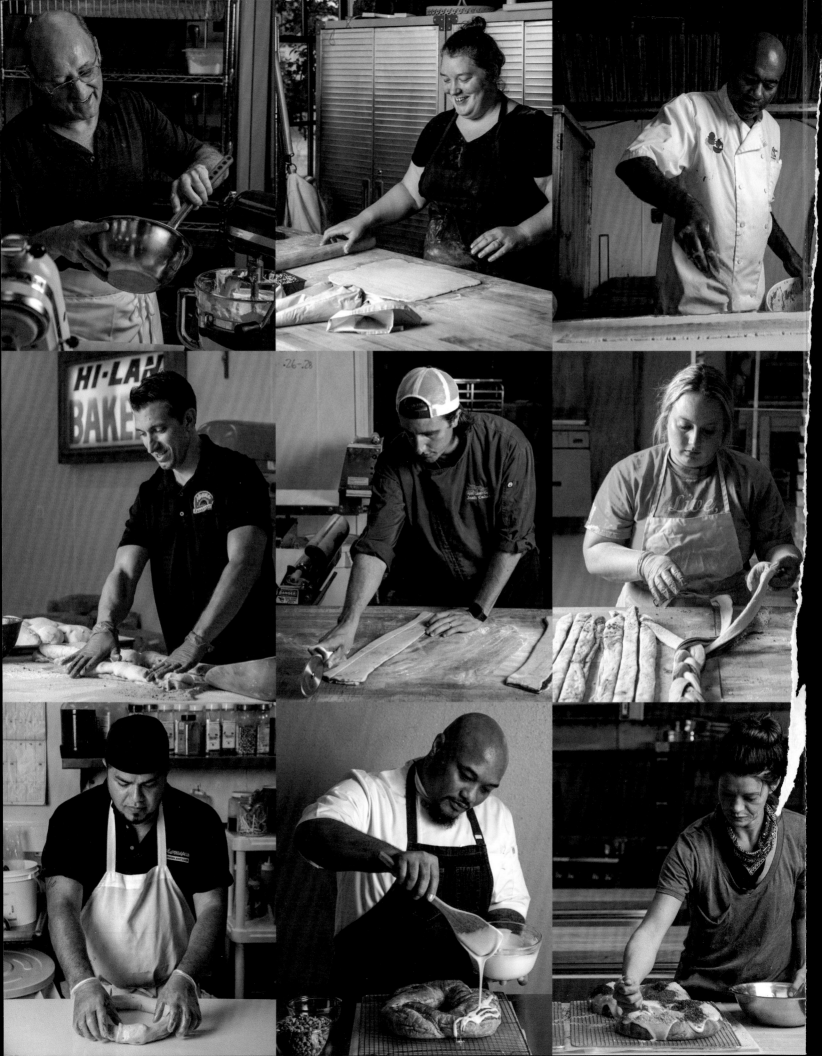

You've Read About Thousands of Years of King Cake, Now Make One Yourself!

This NOCHI King Cake recipe is courtesy of the New Orleans Culinary & Hospitality Institute.

START BY MAKING THE CINNAMON FILLING.

⅓ cup butter
⅓ cup brown sugar
1 tbsp all-purpose flour
1 tbsp cinnamon
1 tbsp honey
½ egg (reserve the other half for the dough)
¼ tsp vanilla extract

- Melt the butter.
- Pour the melted butter into a bowl and mix with the brown sugar until well combined.
- Add the flour, cinnamon, and honey. Mix well.
- Add the eggs and vanilla extract. Mix well.
- Cover and place in the refrigerator until ready to use.

NEXT, IT'S TIME TO MAKE YOUR KING CAKE DOUGH.

2 ½ cups bread flour
¾ tsp yeast, instant or rapid rise
3 tbsp + 1 tsp sugar
1 tsp salt
⅓ cup butter
1 ½ eggs
½ tsp honey
⅔ cup milk

- Place all dough ingredients in a large bowl. Make sure butter is soft.
- Mix ingredients on low speed using a stand mixer for 4 minutes until well combined. If you don't have a mixer, that's also fine; you'll just need more elbow grease.
- Next, mix ingredients on medium speed for approximately 6 minutes. To check if the dough is ready, tear off a small piece. You should be able to stretch it thin enough to see light coming through without the dough tearing.
- Cover the bowl with plastic wrap or a clean dishtowel and set aside for 30 minutes to begin proofing the dough.
- Transfer the dough to a floured surface and roll into a rectangle with 1 inch thickness.

- Move the dough to a tray or baking sheet and cover it with plastic wrap. Place it in the refrigerator overnight to continue proofing.
- When you are ready to bake, remove the dough from the refrigerator and let it sit for 30 minutes.
- Roll the dough into a rectangle (approximately 20 x 8 inches).
- Spread the cinnamon filling on the rectangle and fold in half lengthwise. Your folded dough should be approximately 20 x 4 inches.
- Cut the dough into 3 even strips lengthwise.
- Stretch the strips to 24 inches each. Braid the 3 pieces, then shape into a circle or oval.
- Line a baking sheet with parchment paper and place the unbaked cake on it.
- Cover and set aside in a warm place for approximately 1.5 hours, or until it's nearly double its size (for home bakers, a good trick is to place the unbaked cake on the middle rack of an oven that's off. Place a pan of hot water on the oven floor).
- Bake at 325°F until golden brown or until the cake is at an internal temperature of 190°F. This will be approximately 12 to 15 minutes in a convection oven or approximately 20 minutes in a regular oven.

FINALLY, EVERYONE'S FAVORITE PART— ICING AND DECORATING!

2 cups powdered sugar
¼ cup whole milk
1 tsp vanilla extract
Sugar and food coloring as desired
Small plastic baby

- Combine powdered sugar, whole milk, and vanilla extract in a bowl. Mix until smooth and set side.
- To make colored sugars, put sugar into three bowls— one for purple, another for green, and a third for gold. Start with a few drops of coloring, mixing until incorporated. Add more, a few drops at a time, until your sugar is the desired color.
- Once the cake has cooled, lift the cake and insert the baby into the bottom for the future queen or king to find.
- Drizzle the icing over the cake.
- Sprinkle sugar on top, alternating between the three colors.
- Eat and repeat.

Bakery Index